WRESTLING *with* ANGELS

JOHN HANRAHAN
WRESTLING *with* ANGELS

A True Story of Addiction, Resurrection, Hope, Fashion, Training Celebrities, and Man's Oldest Sport

RARE BIRD
LOS ANGELES, CALIF.

THIS IS A GENUINE RARE BIRD BOOK

Rare Bird
453 South Spring Street, Suite 302
Los Angeles, CA 90013
rarebirdbooks.com

FIRST HARDCOVER EDITION

Set in Minion
Printed in the United States

10 9 8 7 6 5 4 3 2 1

Publisher's Cataloging-in-Publication Data

Names: Hanrahan, John M., author.
Title: Wrestling with Angels: A True Story of Addiction, Resurrection, Hope, Fashion, Training Celebrities, and Man's Oldest Sport / John Hanrahan.
Description: First Hardcover Edition | A Genuine Rare Bird Book | New York, NY; Los Angeles, CA: Rare Bird Books, 2020.
Identifiers: ISBN: 9781644281147
Subjects: LCSH Hanrahan, John, author. | Wrestlers—United States—Biography. | Athletes—United States—Biography. | Models (Persons)—United States—Biography. | Personal trainers—Biography. | Fathers and sons—Biography. | Drug addicts—United States—Biography. | Drug addicts—Family relationships—United States. | BISAC BIOGRAPHY & AUTOBIOGRAPHY / Personal Memoirs | BIOGRAPHY & AUTOBIOGRAPHY / Sports
Classification: LCC GV331.H36 2020 | DDC 613.7/1092—dc23

This book is dedicated to my family, and to all the families across the nation that have endured and are enduring the challenges of addiction. It is my hope that this book's honest portrayal of a personal perspective, as well as a loving parent's perspective, will help to provide hope and inspiration to those families to never give up. To those who are no longer here—including Gerry Harrington, who suffered but also helped countless others with his generous spirit of hope and healing—this book is my prayer that those suffering gain the strength to conquer their challenges and that those who have lost loved ones know that their prayers were not unheard.

THE END & THE BEGINNING
"Have you planned his funeral?"

THAT'S WHAT THE DOCTOR said: *Have you planned his funeral?*

He said this to us in a matter-of-fact way. Because it was pretty much a fact: Connor, our son, our firstborn, just nineteen years old, had been laid to waste by addiction.

Kirsten and I looked at the doctor and then turned to Connor, who sat silently. I looked closely at him. He was my son, but he wasn't Connor anymore. He was a shell of his former self. The morning Connor arrived, clouds shrouded the sky but a light of purity radiated from his eyes. In that moment it was as if the Creator had lifted a veil and reminded me of the all-fulfilling love that I had been shown years earlier in a dark period of my life. Light danced playfully around baby Connor's face. There was no light or energy around him now. I didn't think it was possible, but he looked worse than the skeleton we'd picked up at the airport a few days before. The cold fluorescent bulbs of the office made his face look pale yellow, jaundiced from Hepatitis C. His eye sockets were dark and seemingly bruised, like he was in a fight, a fight he was losing .

We knew what was going on. Knew the doctor had seen too many cases like his. Knew he was right that Connor was on borrowed time. Knew he was trying to scare Connor straight. Knew the Connor we knew was in there, trapped, fighting for his life. Knew he was not giving up.

But how much fight did he have left in him?

Have you planned his funeral? Because he's going to die. My son. The addict.

With no hope coming from the doctor, Kirsten and I looked into each other's eyes for the hope we longed for. But we were just numb. We had endured this pain for so long. The boomerang of Connor's addiction had left us spiritually, emotionally, and financially drained. All we had left was our faith, but even that was waning, and the stress threatened to rip our family apart for good.

It all happened so fast. In the middle of high school, Connor said he wanted to try wrestling, which thrilled me. I had been a state champion wrestler in high school and the winningest wrestler in Penn State history after my four years on the NCAA mats. I had challenged some of the greats in the sport, trained for the Olympics, and even won tournaments against champs half my age after my kids were born. But I never pushed Connor or my younger son, Liam, into wrestling or any sport. Connor hadn't wrestled since he was a little kid, but he made the decision to try out anyway. He made the team.

Then, at one of his matches, he got slammed and ended up breaking his leg. He was put on painkillers, and so it began: prescription became addiction, and Connor soon found himself seeking out more pills on the streets. They weren't hard to find where we lived, in north suburban Atlanta. They hadn't been hard to find anywhere we'd lived. But it wasn't just a fight against pills now. Connor's addiction had quickly evolved to heroin. That's what happens when people like Connor can't find or afford the pills anymore: they buy a heroin shot on the street for five bucks. The scourge of our nation is cheaper than a six-pack of beer.

Connor knew kids who had overdosed and died from heroin. His good friend was found overdosed with a needle stuck in his arm in the basement of his parents' home. It didn't stop him from using. And we never saw it until it was too late.

Have you planned his funeral?

The doctor's words echoed in our heads. Kirsten and I mustered the energy for what we believed would be one last time—one last chance for Connor to stay clean. He had been hospitalized, sent to residential treatment centers, lived in intensive outpatient sober living homes, completed an outpatient program, moved across the country for a change of scenery and to try a new program. Now, at our wits' end, we were taking him to a methadone clinic.

Every week we put Connor and a clunky toolbox outfitted with a silver padlock into the car. He lugged the box into the clinic, where the nurse administered that day's dose and then placed the rest of the week's supply in the box for Connor to take at home. She watched as Connor locked the box and left the clinic.

We thought it was working. Believed it was working. Wanted to believe it was working. Connor's liver enzymes even went up a bit, but this was before there was a cure for Hep C, and when his enzymes dropped again, he collapsed. We brought him to the emergency room, where he stayed for two weeks. He needed a liver transplant. The doctor at the hospital told us if he did this again, he was dead. *We know*, we said, *we are trying to get his enzymes up*. We thought, believed, wanted to believe he was just talking about the Hep C. We had thought, believed, wanted to believe the methadone was working.

Turned out Connor was still using. After all we had been through and continued to go through, after all we missed and vowed never to miss again, we still didn't see it. How many times had I denied he could possibly have a problem, even when Connor didn't try to hide it? Early in his using, I found him passed out in the hall in the middle of the night and thought maybe he was just exhausted, or at worst, learning a typical teenage lesson from drinking too much. He said he needed to go to the hospital, and I said, *Get up. You're okay*. I didn't know what was going on. I didn't want to know. I was insensitive to his complaints, I figured he was faking an illness. That's what I believed. That's what I told Connor. Even when he told me that his chest hurt. I dismissed that as the phantom pain of the hypochondriac he wasn't, instead of the addict he was.

I never took Connor to the hospital that night. I learned later that he had mixed opiates and amphetamines in excess and the combination had made him feel like something was wrong in his heart. He was seventeen years old and had been using for more than a year.

I denied the truth. Maybe because we had settled in suburban Atlanta, where you don't think about the problems behind the manicured lawns and nice front doors. Maybe he was hiding it well behind his good grades and friends who looked anything but shady, as if only shady kids use during the opioid crisis that still haunts us today. Maybe I simply did not want to admit it—like so many parents who live in denial and lie to themselves.

Maybe all that would be true for most parents. But it shouldn't have been for me.

As Connor sat in his hospital bed, I knew I had not done everything to help him. I was living with more than just denial of Connor's addiction—more than fear of Connor's death. I was hiding something from him and his brother Liam, as I had from almost everyone in my life for decades: my story. *My whole story*. The one that I always wanted to tell, but the few times I tried, I failed. The parts of my story that made me feel weak. The parts that made me feel like a loser no matter how much I won.

Here's the story Connor and most everyone around me knew. My name is John Hanrahan, and in 1960, I arrived in this world the fifth born and first son of six Hanrahan children, a typical suburban American Irish Catholic family in Falls Church, Virginia. I was a nationally acclaimed high school wrestler who earned a scholarship to Penn State, where I was the first to win one hundred matches. While I was in college, I became an accidental model when I was discovered by a prominent agent, who caught one of my matches while channel surfing his Manhattan Cable. I became a top model for the Ford Agency in New York City and the worldwide face of Versace for one season. After my modeling career ended, I became a trainer to the stars and worked with the biggest names in show business: Rod Stewart, Julia Roberts, Natasha Richardson, Tim Burton, Patricia Heaton, Joan Lunden, Howard Stern, Diane Sawyer, Sandy Gallin, David Geffen, Cindy Lauper, Annabella Sciorra, Tara Reid, Mary McCormack, Rosie O'Donnell…

Here's the story Connor and most everyone around me did not know. I was a drug addict. I had been addicted to cocaine—an addiction I had hidden behind my successes. An addiction that my parents had been as blind to when I was in high school and college as I had been to Connor's. My name is John Hanrahan, and I was an addict. And am an addict. An addiction I never fully confronted until the day Connor was born.

But that was not all of it. I was still doing what I had done for more than thirty years: hiding the whole story, instead of confronting it and putting it out there for Connor, so he would know I understood what he was going through more than I ever wanted to admit. I would fear that truth no more. This moment would begin my full redemption in the light for all to see.

I looked at Connor and told him I understood his doctor's words better than he could possibly imagine. *Have you planned his funeral?* No, because I knew Connor could beat this, even this close to death. Because I had seen death myself.

My name is John Hanrahan, and in October 1985, I died on the floor of my neighbor's apartment, after a lethal drug injection that ended my life as I knew it.

PART I

LIFE & DEATH & LIFE

ALL-AMERICAN BOY

I WAS A CHILD of the sixties, growing up in a large Irish Catholic family. My mother was kind, my father no-nonsense, my older sisters caring, and my younger brother the kid I needed to protect.

Born in the Bronx, my dad left home at seventeen, joined the Marines, and fought at Iwo Jima and Saipan. After the war, he married my mom, earned his PhD in electrical engineering, and got a job at the Naval Research Laboratory working on top-secret projects during the beginning of the Cold War. But that was hardly extraordinary. Our Falls Church, Virginia, suburb was just over the bridge from Washington, DC. Everyone knew someone working on some top-secret government project during the Cold War. My dad had lost his father at a young age, and the thought of losing the security that he provided was unimaginable.

Like other families in the 1960s, we cried in shock over the Kennedy assassination (which I barely understood) and while watching the DC riots (which I couldn't understand). Like every kid I knew, I had accidents, illnesses, run-ins with my siblings, prayed with my family, went to church, and hated school, especially the strict Catholic school I started in first grade and the nun who taught my class. I was painfully shy and constantly fidgety, which drew the Sister's ire, and that only made me more self-conscious.

Where I wasn't self-conscious was on the playground. I played "football" with the boys on the blacktop with a tennis ball, and it quickly became the only thing I wanted to do at school. I loved getting physical and discovering what my body could do. I got nicknamed "Powerhouse" because I could continue carrying the ball with five kids piled on me. My mom was constantly patching my Zaire-blue trouser knees after I dragged them along the asphalt. Every hole made me feel more complete, more like myself.

I graduated to organized football later that fall. Mr. Stevenson, our neighbor who ran a Texaco filling station, would pile kids in the back of his pickup truck and take us to the local high school to play on a boys' club team. By second grade, football had given me all the confidence that I never had in school. I acquired a reputation for breaking the facemasks on my helmet because I hit with my head so hard. I never got to run or throw the ball, but I didn't care about that, or that the coaches' kids got to play glamour positions like quarterback and running back. I played the line on offense, running guys over, and on defense tackling the other teams' glamour boys. I was happy in the trenches. I was happy hitting people hard, and when they passed around the second grade boys' winter club flyer at school that fall, I rushed home and told my mom I knew exactly what I wanted to learn next: boxing.

Oh, honey. Why don't you try wrestling?

But I want to do boxing!

She took the flyer, looked it over, and shook her head.

No, honey. Not boxing. Try wrestling.

I pleaded my case, but she held firm, telling me how she had attended a college wrestling match on a date at the Naval Academy and loved it. I pushed, but I could tell Mom thought wrestling was a higher-class sport than boxing.

Mom was right, of course. I might have had nothing more to write about if I hadn't relented and started wrestling when I was seven years old.

Wrestling was everything football wasn't for me, and I took to it immediately. I had felt confident on the football field but never super comfortable in that boys' club. Everyone else always seemed to know more about the game than I did. Coaches spent less time explaining plays and strategies to the line and more time telling us what not to do so the players who mattered most could score. What they told me was something like what you tell the Hulk. *Hanrahan smash!*

Maybe it wasn't just me. It seemed a lot of fathers tutored their kids in football even by first grade. Not my dad. He wasn't an athlete or into sports. He was tough as nails as a Marine, but he was a mathematician now. He wasn't even at many of my games. From the moment I started elementary school, he did not like the idea of me wasting study time playing ball, while I had already made up my mind I was not going to waste time studying when there was ball to be played. I brought schoolbooks home just in case he asked to see them. I tried to trick him into giving me the answers to my homework so I could get back to playing faster. I would come into his den and ask him about questions I hadn't even looked at, thinking I could quickly get all the answers. Instead I ended up spending mind-numbing amounts of time listening to his insights into what the problem really was about or what a book could teach me. I learned to avoid his den. Somehow, I still managed to get good grades.

But wrestling? Wrestling was something I knew I could learn—something I wanted to learn. No one needed to tell me to study harder. Even in second grade, I easily grasped the objectives in front of me—take your opponent down, put him on his back, and stay off your own back—and longed to do it the best I could. The only thing I didn't like about wrestling at first was the way my knees felt on the mat. I had no kneepads, so I wore an old pair of jeans to practice.

That problem solved, I moved onto the bigger problem of the club coach. He knew nothing about the sport and had never wrestled a day in his life. He taught every rule and move from a book. He wasn't going to give me what I needed, and neither was my dad, so I developed my own instinctual methods to knock opponents off their feet and pry them onto their back. This was too much for most of the other club kids, whom I took down one after another. My team even named a move after me: "The Hanrahan Special," in which I grasped my opponent's far ankle while simultaneously trapping his far elbow, sinking my chest back below his torso, and bulldozing forward to knock him on his back. The tackle I had perfected in football served me well too. In wrestling, they called it a double leg takedown.

Wrestling became my own little universe. It gave me everything football, school, and my father could not. From my first matches, I understood the power of imposing my will against another human being. I was a winner. I was unstoppable. I went through my second-grade season the undefeated league champion.

And then in third grade, I lost for the first time—to Matt Ruffing, the son of the league commissioner. Matt didn't pin me, but he beat me in every other way. He was well trained and always steps ahead of me as we fought through positions I did not know were possible. I remember it was loud and I felt like everyone there was against me. My lungs were burning. My mouth was too dry even to spit. The buzzer sounded, reverberating off the gym walls, and that was it. I rose to my feet and stood there humiliated as Matt Ruffing's arm was raised, tears streaming down my face.

That Matt Ruffing and I continued to tangle and I later had my share of victories against him did nothing to undo how I felt that night. I felt alone. Because I was alone. In wrestling, there are no teammates to hide behind. My father was in the bleachers, but that was no comfort. I had no idea what the word vulnerable meant then, but that's what I was, standing there in defeat for the first time. I already knew fear. I began having night terrors when I was seven. My sister Teri would come to me in the middle of the night and calm me down by rubbing my hands. Feeling this vulnerable was worse. I had no control over what I saw in my dreams, but I had control over how I performed on the mat. Now I had a new fear, the fear of losing, and I would do everything I could to ensure it never happened again.

Because wrestling made me feel alive. Complete. Like a winner. Smart and capable of learning from my mistakes. Powerful. I bought a set of weights with the money I'd saved up. My dad shook his head disapprovingly. He thought I would just lift and look at myself in the mirror. He saw it as ego. I know he only wanted to make sure I was doing things for the right reasons, but it hurt that he didn't understand me. I was on my way to becoming a state champion—I knew it and had the record and work ethic to prove it. Still, he made me explain my motives.

The last thing I want to do is lift weights, Dad. But you know what? I want to be the best wrestler I can be, and this is part of the equation.

Dad walked away, which only made me push harder. By my eighth-grade season, I was a junior champion and had an open invitation to the varsity wrestling practice. It was tortuous and painful, but I figured it built character—something the coach always talked about. Besides, I desperately wanted to be a part of his team and wrestle under the spotlights for the Falls Church High School Jaguars. They had a great wrestling tradition, perennially ranked as one of the top teams in the state, while the basketball team sucked. The school packed them in for home meets to capacity crowds all winter long. As the varsity team prepared to enter, the houselights would shut off and the spotlights flared up the circle of the mat as the Doobie Brothers' "Black Water" would echo through the gym. The team would bang the double doors loudly and then burst into the spotlights. There was nothing cooler in my mind.

Wrestling: what men do during boys' basketball season. *This is where I'm meant to be*, I thought. At the same time, I literally got a whiff of what else was to come. Because just after I became a junior champion, I smelled drugs for the first time.

EVERYTHING BEGINS

THE SUMMER IT HAPPENED, I was with my best friend Burt, who lived next door.

Burt and I had a long history of making our own trouble. We'd do anything for fun, even mess with my grandfather, Big Daddy. Big Daddy was a big man and a hard drinker who lived on the other side of us in a house he built with his friends. He would pay me and Burt to collect bottles and broken glass off his property and around the creek that ran behind our houses. That got boring fast, so Burt and I got the idea to break any whole bottles we found against the rocks in the creek and then bring Big Daddy a bucket load of broken glass. When we showed up that day with only shards and cuts on our hands, Big Daddy paid us and then fired us.

Burt and I didn't care. We were in it together. We stayed friends even after I broke his two front teeth playing hot potato with a heavy plastic wind-up Milton Bradley toy called Time Bomb, and my parents had to pay for his new teeth. We were still best friends in eighth grade, exploring the woods near the field where we played pickup football games, when we stumbled upon a big metal tackle box under a bush.

We opened it and found it packed with drugs—pot, hashish, pills—and a syringe. We had no idea exactly what those things were, and any interest we had in finding out ourselves was trumped by our sense that they were bad and, most importantly, valuable. This is not to pretend that I was a golden child before this moment, or that I'd never felt the temptation to try something. After class one day in sixth grade, a bunch of us stole some liquor and got drunk for the first time in my friend Rocky's basement. I staggered home, only stopping on the hill between our house and the church, where the world spun and I puked my guts out. I made it home in time for dinner with no repercussions, the advantage of getting lost in a family of six children.

But as Burt and I looked at the tackle box, money was on our minds, not mischief. We thought there might be a reward for finding the box and turning it in. We took the box to Burt's mom, who called the police. When the officer arrived and saw what we'd found, he said how proud he was of us. Drugs were bad, and maybe we helped save a life. He explained what each of the pills were and then clipped a bud of marijuana on a pair of hemostats and burned it with his lighter so we could know what it smelled like and could steer clear of it.

We told him we would. It smelled nasty to me anyway. We didn't get a reward. Still, we felt like heroes. But that wasn't the hero I wanted to be. I wanted to be a hero on the mat.

My idol was a wrestler named Dan Gable, and that summer after eighth grade was the first time I saw him—and real wrestling—on TV at the 1972 Olympics in Munich, Germany. I remember excitedly tuning the antenna on the television in the family den, trying to get the ABC broadcast. The black-and-white picture stayed fuzzy, but it was clear enough to see the athletes in their singlets battling it out in front of a packed arena. I pulled the straps of my own singlet over my favorite wrestling T-shirt and sat ready to follow all the action.

That's when I saw him: Dan Gable. I'd only read about him in a book—the first one I'd ever gotten from the library, and to be honest the only one I had ever read cover to cover. I knew all about his work ethic and dedication. I knew about his pain: how he came home from high school one day in Iowa and discovered his sister on the living room floor, raped and murdered. I saw in his every move how his anger fueled him, unleashing an unmatched intensity as he ripped through his Olympic opponents. He won the gold medal without allowing a point to be scored on him.

That is going to be me one day.

Shortly after Gable's victory, the entire Olympic broadcast changed. Jim McKay interrupted images of the thrill of victory, agony of defeat, and spirit of sportsmanship that defines the best of humankind with reports of extreme violence that mark our worst. The screen cut away to images of the Olympic Village where, McKay reported, a Palestinian terrorist group called Black September had taken Israeli Olympians hostage. At least one had been killed trying to help his teammates, who remained captive. It affected me deeply as an athlete who aspired to be on an Olympic podium one day.

The next day, against the backdrop of terror, the broadcast returned to the Olympic wrestling venue and showed a young American wrestler named Rick Sanders, who wrestled like an artist. Fluid and creative with his movements, he made me realize that wrestling can truly be artistic and lethal. His matches inspired me and allowed me to forget about the human tragedy that was still unfolding—but only for a moment. The broadcast was again interrupted with McKay reporting live.

We've just gotten the final word. You know, when I was a kid, my father used to say our greatest hopes and our worst fears are seldom realized. Our worst fears have been realized tonight. They've now said that there were eleven hostages. Two were killed in their rooms yesterday morning; nine were killed at the airport tonight. They're all gone.

The senseless violence of the Munich tragedy—men's hate for people not like them—echoed the senseless violence I experienced and also could not understand in my own life.

In seventh grade, I was no longer in Catholic school but bussed to J. G. Whittier Junior High School, a recently integrated school in the same neighborhood as T. C. Williams High School, which had its racial tensions captured in the movie *Remember the Titans*. The movie told the story of how the school's football team overcame its own racial bias and hate in their hearts. They began to appreciate one another and destroy their opponents, who often continued to spew hate as TC went on to win the state championship.

Despite that victory, tensions remained high, as they had since the DC riots of 1968. We were integrated but not together. Every morning after the buses arrived, white kids would gather on one side of the lobby and black kids on the other. Most mornings, I hid my 85-pound frame behind Charlie, a 280-pound wrestler who lived on my block and had been held back, which made him even bigger than the biggest kids. Charlie knew me as a "little" wrestler, and he let me stay behind him as fights broke out all around us. On a few occasions, the violence was bad enough to close down the school for the day and bus us home.

Despite my wrestling prowess, I avoided fighting anywhere but the mat for three reasons: I was still small, I didn't want to give my dad a reason to put me back in Catholic school, and I had no desire to fight people who I did not hate. In fact, my best friend Floyd was the first black kid I became close to. We knew each other from football before junior high, and I talked him into doing wrestling. Despite our different backgrounds, Floyd became part of my family, and I became part of his, though his chained-up dog, Whitey, never accepted me. Every time Whitey growled at me, Floyd just laughed. *Don't mind her. She just hates white people.*

After a local high school football game one night, racial tensions spilled over into the streets of our town. Floyd's older brother was killed in a hit-and-run that the news attributed to racism. It was as senseless and tragic as the Munich Massacre unfolding that summer. It all left me confused, nervous, and unsettled.

A few days later, we learned of more death in the shadow of the Olympic tragedy. Rick Sanders had left Munich, silver medal around his neck and girlfriend on his arm, and started hitchhiking through Eastern Europe. His body had been found along the road, apparently run over by a truck. His bag contained his red USA Olympic team pants and jacket and six dollars. His Olympic silver medal was never recovered.

Reports of Sanders' end affected my wrestling brotherhood deeply. The older wrestlers from my neighborhood told us younger ones incredible stories about him, how he was known for partying but could still wipe the mat with anyone in the wrestling room. One kid said he'd heard that when Sanders hadn't shown at the Munich arena on match day, the coaches found him in a bar. Rick Sanders wasn't hiding the hard partying side of his life from anyone. But by this time, I was.

If anything marks the beginning of what I call my double life of addiction to wrestling and drugs, it's the summer I saw Dan Gable wrestle—the first time I tried marijuana. Not six months after I promised that cop I wouldn't.

The summer before my freshman year of high school, I found myself sitting on the railroad ties near the Falls Church community center pool with a bunch of the wilder, cooler, older kids in town. My life revolved around that pool in the summers throughout high school, and that life had now spilled over into the woods and these tracks, where kids drank and smoked pot seemingly every day. I had some status as a wrestler and football player, but I wasn't part of their crowd. They wanted me to join them and were passing a pipe down the line. The smell the officer had showed us was getting closer.

I had meant it when I told him I wouldn't do it. I told myself I wouldn't do it. I wouldn't succumb to peer pressure.

Here... No thanks. *Come on...* Nah, I'm good. *HERE...*

This didn't sound like a request anymore, but a do-it-and-you're-in, don't-and-you're-out ultimatum. These weren't my friends. These were the kids I desperately wanted to accept me—and they weren't taking no for an answer.

They knew it was my first time. Embarrassment and fear of being called a loser overtook my conscience. I took a toke and got immediate praise, which I accepted. On the inside, I knew I had just made a mistake—that I had betrayed that police officer, my parents, and myself.

Not that I let those feelings stop me. I drank and smoked pot that entire summer with my new friends. We stole beer from the 7–11 or High's. We partied though the night. Thus began my double life: one "me" riding around with kids in cars, drinking, smoking, and eventually doing harder drugs, the other "me" maintaining the facade of "All-American Boy"—the wrestler with the bright future.

My double life was really only for my family and teachers. I didn't have to hide it from the wrestlers. Rick Sanders wasn't an exception in the sport. Wrestlers are the ultimate athletes and party animals—a fact my sister Teri confirmed for me on New Year's Eve my freshman year. She had a date with the greatest wrestler to ever come out of our area, who was on break from his college wrestling team in Indiana. They let me tag along with them to a house party. I was the youngest one there, and they took me under their wing and taught me how to do tequila shots. While they left me to go dance, I stayed in the kitchen doing shots until after the clock struck twelve. When we returned home, Teri's date deposited me on the side of the house, where I remained until I puked. I slept in the side yard—and I still woke up and completed a three-hour 8:00 a.m. wrestling practice.

I figured Rick Sanders would've been proud, especially because I was playing with the big boys now on every level. Nothing was going to keep me out of that spotlight. I longed to be there. I worked my ass off to get there. I may have been smoking pot and drinking. I may have been awkward around girls. But all those Johns bowed before John the Wrestler. I felt more confident and more alive than ever when I was on the wrestling mat.

My freshman year, I won the varsity starting position at my weight in a wrestle-off against a kid from the neighborhood, whom I knew from my all-star boys' club team that competed around the DC metro area. I won the girl too: captain of the freshman cheerleaders, whom I'd had a crush on since first grade. But things were not meant to end the way they started. In wrestling, the coach could allow someone to challenge for the starting position, and I ended up losing a challenge match after a controversial call. I lost the girl soon after.

Fair or not, I resolved never to let that happen again. Despite my status as the backup 112-pounder, my high school coach took me to the NCAA nationals, and I got to meet my hero Dan Gable in the practice room. Clinging to the confidence wrestling gave me, I didn't just gawk from afar or ask to shake his hand—I walked right up to him, announced who I was, and asked him to "go takedowns with me." He looked at me and said... Nah, that's okay, kid.

Dejected, I sat against the wall and watched him work out. When it was over, he came up to me, grabbed me by the arm, and said, "Let's go." We playfully went at it for over twenty minutes, and he even let me ask questions about technique. I thanked him. Hungry for more, I went looking for another top-level wrestler to work out with. That summer I attended summer camp with Doug Blubaugh, an Olympic champion and college coach who taught me how "those who do, do." His words still in my head, I became determined to do.

Sophomore year, I regained the starting position, and there was no taking my spot away again. I won the bronze medal at State and was now one of the leaders of the team. I moved up to a higher-tier cheerleader too—I was now dating the captain of the varsity squad.

Nothing could stop me. Except me.

BEING WATCHED

UNTIL APRIL OF MY sophomore year, my biggest anxiety was the future. Wrestling gave me confidence on the mat, but at night, especially before the season and after it ended, I would lie in bed, unable to sleep. I was scared that I'd have nowhere to go. That I would pick the wrong path. That I would be beholden to my parents forever. That they would spend their hard-earned savings sending me to college, and I would screw up and have to come home and remain in Falls Church and live under their roof, bound by their rules. The loser drunk stoner child.

Nothing I did—including drinking, getting high more, or getting into the occasional fight—made things any clearer. They only made me forget. As soon as I was sober or the adrenaline wore off or I was alone again, the anxiety returned.

By high school, it seemed to me that everyone knew where he or she was going but me. My friends were getting ready to enter their family businesses, which we didn't have, or knew exactly what career they'd pursue. I took a career aptitude test, and it recommended that I become a funeral director.

My father wasn't much help in guiding me. It wasn't just the top-secret nature of his work. I asked him once what I should be, and he responded that not many men get to make a living doing something they enjoy, and I "gotta work"—which meant study. Which I was not about to do. I saw no value in learning math or science. Art and English bored me. I hated it all, though I still managed to get A's and B's simply by looking the part of the conscientious student, respectful and seemingly attentive.

Thank God for wrestling. Whenever I stepped in the training room or competed with the team, I felt like I belonged, like everything would be okay. It anchored me while allowing me to be the free spirit I longed to be everywhere else in my life. Wrestling was my creative expression, my science, and unlike my schoolwork, I continued to work hard and take beating after beating to get better. My teammates never knew what happened after I got home and crawled into my bed at night, separated from the wrestling and partying, when the anxiety would creep in.

That anxiety diminished on April 5, 1976—the day I got my first letter from a college. It was from Washington and Lee University, a terrific liberal arts school a few hours from us in Virginia. They spelled my name wrong, but what did that matter? Their wrestling coach had seen me capture my State medal, and while there was no mention of a scholarship, my coach said it was implied, assuming I continued to excel on the mat and managed to graduate. He also said this was just the beginning.

Johnny, you are being watched.

And oh, how I wanted that scholarship. I was a shaky investment, but this one letter made me believe I was going to be able to take care of myself on my own terms. *I want to pay my own way through college with a scholarship,* I said to myself over and over. A free ride would free me to make my own mistakes without my parents paying for them. My dad would never get to question my grades and say, "Why did you get a D in this class? I'm paying for this."

The letter from Washington and Lee was enough to keep my anxiety at bay, and I worked even harder to see how much better I could do and how high I could climb. I made the national junior team and got to compete in Poland, which was then behind the Iron Curtain my dad was working to bring down. At our first training center in Warsaw, we shared showers with the Polish women's basketball team. They were excited about our American shampoo, and we were excited to be showering in the same room with six-foot-tall women! My teenage boy hormones appreciated that moment, but the rest of the trip only made me appreciate what I had in America. All I wanted to represent was a symbol of our country's freedom and capitalism. My American wrestling dream.

We took a team bus through the countryside, passing farms that looked stuck in the previous century, until we reached the small town of Sieradz where we completed our training. We had plenty of Polish money, or złoty, but there was nothing to buy. We were hungry and tired of food like stomach soup and tongue, which was probably delicious to the locals but wasn't exactly McDonald's to a fifteen-year-old suburban kid from America. Desperate for something to eat and the comforts of home, we found an ice cream shop one night, but it only sold small individual cones, so we went to a hardware store and bought a bucket and paid to fill it with ice cream. The next day, we left for home, and I actually kissed the ground upon landing in the US. Then I went and found my friends and spent the rest of the summer drinking and smoking, which continued right into my junior year.

In high school, I'd stop drinking and smoking pot in season, but in the offseason I'd continue to train while partying. I'd smoke in the morning before school, at lunchtime, and after school. So did many of my teammates. We saw it as a badge of honor if you could wrestle, and even more so if you could wrestle and also party like an animal. In Falls Church, it wasn't a big deal to become a state champion wrestler. But to achieve it while also being a top party animal gave you the highest esteem. We played hard and partied hard, like we heard Rick Sanders had, always trying to outdo each other. Our credo was, "It's one thing to experience wrestling and do everything right and be good at it, but it's another to experience life and be good at it."

And I was. I won the Virginia state tournaments in my weight class the next two years and was the runner-up in my junior year at the AAU Nationals. As I won, college letters kept coming, along with phone calls. Scholarship offers poured in. Coaches visited my parents' living room. They came to school and pulled me out of the classroom. They watched matches under the spotlights, impressed with my performance in front of rabid crowds. They offered me all-expense-paid visits to their schools. The NCAA allowed me to take five of those visits, and I availed myself of all of them.

First up was Michigan State. Though I had been drinking for years, I remember how mature I felt flying alone for the first time, ordering a beer from the Eastern Airline stewardess (I was eighteen, the legal age for drinking beer in Virginia back then), and looking out the window as we passed over my neighborhood upon takeoff.

I didn't like Michigan State, but two things made the visit memorable. First, when I arrived at the airport in DC, I passed a newsstand and saw my current girlfriend, who happened to be a Ford Agency model, looking back at me from the cover of *Washingtonian* magazine. I still smelled like her from the night before! Second, I found myself in the company of many other top recruits. The university was hosting a battle between the USA Olympians and the mighty Soviets. I was staying on the same hotel floor as the Soviet team, and I am not sure what impressed me more: how they dominated our wrestlers, or how much they smoked and drank after doing so. These guys were bad dudes—communists, but still my kind of bad dudes. Wrestlers.

After Michigan State, I visited Indiana State. I went because it was close to Indiana University, where I wanted to visit a girl I liked, and I couldn't afford to get there on my own. I drove to University of Maryland, because my dad was once a professor there, and nearby George Mason University, where the coach offered me an MG sports car to accept their offer to be an anchor for their new program. But I wasn't interested in either of them. I loved Clemson, where they took me waterskiing and then to a disco and introduced me to the drunken crowd on the light-up dance floor. The University of Tennessee, where all the athletes lived in a tower with an amazing mess hall that served prime rib, also impressed me. I had pretty much settled on those two when my coach stopped me after school and told me another opportunity had come up, a big one. Penn State—the biggest wrestling power east of the Mississippi and the most dominant university in the most dominant wrestling state in the country—had called him. They were very interested in me.

One problem: they didn't send a plane ticket. Instead they wanted me to drive four hours with my parents and stay the weekend. I'm not sure what I felt was the bigger slight: not flying me up, or having me bring my mom and dad. I was eighteen and had done all my visits solo so far. To me, it meant that I was an afterthought. I resigned myself to going—it was Penn State after all. I'd drive up in my parents' station wagon. But I was *not* going to bring my parents. In the backseat were my cooler of beer and my bong. Riding shotgun was my oldest friend from public school and my wrestling teammate, Floyd. We had remained best friends since junior high, and while his dog Whitey still hated me, times had changed at school. As seniors, Floyd was voted "Friendliest" and I was named "Foxiest."

It wasn't hard to convince him to come along. I found him in the cafeteria and said something like: *Floyd, come on! I've got the wagon with beer and weed and we're going to Penn State to stay in a hotel while they show me around the school for the weekend. I'm not going to go there, but we might as well have some fun saying no!*

I think he was in the car before I was. Road trip!

As soon as we got through the mountains of Pennsylvania and arrived in the Happy Valley, I realized why they asked me to drive: there was no major airport in this town. I softened my stance a little, and then a little more when I met one of the coaches, a two-time national champion. Coach also seemed amused that I brought my friend Floyd instead of my parents.

We headed over to the weight room to meet the Nittany Lion wrestlers. The first guy introduced to us was Dan. Dan seemed unintimidating—big hips but slight upper body—but Floyd and I knew we shouldn't underestimate him. We had seen him wrestle a few months back, against the University of Maryland. Dan seemed surprisingly relaxed given his opponent was a beast, pacing back and forth behind his bench like a bull.

He slayed the bull that night, but tonight Dan saw only bullshit. He looked disgusted that he'd been assigned to babysit a recruit for the weekend. I told him not to bother, that we would show ourselves around. We had a cooler of beer and a bag of weed in the car to keep us company, and I wasn't going to Penn State without a full out-of-state scholarship. Dan was taken aback by my bravado but warmed to the beer and weed.

Next thing I knew, we were at Dan's fraternity house, which could have been used as the set of *Animal House*—the film came out that same year—with Big Dan a perfect fit for the John Belushi role. *Hey, get a load of this recruit. He brought up his buddy and a case of beer.* After a few beers and bong hits, someone said we should all go over to the Rec Hall wrestling room, where I ended up challenging Dan and a few seniors in my weight class. I did more than hold my own. Dan was completely won over, and I was too. I wanted to go to Penn State—if I got that scholarship.

I felt a connection that day I hadn't at Clemson or Tennessee. I found myself drawn to more than wrestlers, parties, women, and the world-famous Rec Hall. I liked the fact that there were so many colleges and major options within the university. Yes, me: the kid who hadn't read a book since sixth grade. When I told them I wanted to consider photography as a major, the coaching staff set up a meeting for me with the head of the photography department. Floyd and I spent the rest of the weekend bouncing between raucous parties at the frat house and winning over the team's incoming head coach, Rich Lorenzo, at white tablecloth meals at the Nittany Lion Inn. I told him I loved the school and wanted to be a part of their great tradition, competing for a team where matches were packed with fans and where my hard work would be appreciated and honored. But I needed that full ride. The following day, he called with the offer.

Almost two years after I got my first college offer, I signed my letter of intent and became a Nittany Lion wrestler. That summer, I embraced that new identity as I prepared to make my last stand for Falls Church and win the high school national tournament in Iowa City, the tournament I had been runner-up in as a junior. I decided to skip my training in Falls Church and drove up to Happy Valley, with my throwing dummy "Bill" riding shotgun this time instead of Floyd. I was ready to work hard and party hard with Dan, who nicknamed me "Boy Wonder."

I fell just short again in Iowa City. Dan was there to watch the matches and saw me make a great run through the Greco-Roman bracket, even beating the number-one "Dream Team" recruit from Kansas in the semifinals. In the national finals, however, I butted heads with my opponent from Illinois and split my head open above my eye. It got taped up enough for me to finish the match, but I lost, collecting another national runner-up award before heading to the hospital to get stitched up. The doctor advised me to withdraw from the Freestyle event that evening. But instead of returning to the arena to bow out, Dan took me to a bar downtown.

The beer helped to relieve some of the pain—as did all the old guys around us telling their wrestling stories, especially the one about an Iowa wrestler who lost a bet in this bar and had to strip naked and swim up the river outside. Dan and I were laughing. Offhand, I started joking that I never officially withdrew from the Freestyle tournament. They were going to be calling my name soon for the first round. I joked I should go back and do that match drunk just for fun.

If you do that, Boy Wonder, that would be wild.

I did it. Because that's what wrestlers do. That's what I do. Wrestling is what soothes me. It is what I run to, not away from.

Dan yelled out to everybody in the bar that I was on deck up at the arena and how I was gonna go kick some ass. Then we took my bruised, stitched up, and boozed-up body back to the arena. I changed back into my black singlet and put on my black wrestling shoes just in time to hear my name called. I'd wrestled drunk before—even at a tournament a few weeks after State, and it hadn't affected me at all. But I had never wrestled with a large swollen gash stitched above my eye. Still, I ended up dominating my opponent from Ohio, getting big throws but cracking heads and opening the gash again. I shook hands, felt my arm raised, and then officially withdrew to avoid risking any permanent damage.

Coach Lorenzo found me and shook my hand, talking about how good I looked and seemingly having no idea I had been drinking before the match. The coach of Team Virginia, however, knew I was smoking—at least after the match. I was the only wrestler to place from Virginia that year, and when the coach looked to congratulate me, he caught me doing a bong hit behind a dumpster. He just laughed. He knew me well, having been my elite boys' club coach and now the coach at George Mason University, which had offered me a full ride to stay in state. He shook his head. *You'll never do anything in college.*

I told myself to remember that when I proved him wrong. I wasn't going to let him spoil my high, and I was high on everything that summer. I decided to get even higher by trying something new: cocaine. Or at least that's how I rationalized it. I didn't think of myself as an alcoholic or a drug addict. People like that couldn't do what I did on the mat. People like that did not win scholarships to Penn State.

No one could stop me. Except me.

I was with my girlfriend, the cover model, who made me a fondue dinner. She lived in an apartment with her mother, who was never home. She had gotten a little coke from her uncle—enough to make me wonder what it would be like to do more. This taste was a tease. It was unlike anything I had ever felt while drinking or smoking. It gave me a feeling of strength that I had only found wrestling up to that point. I was always "foxy" (thanks, yearbook committee), but cocaine pulled me out of my shell and made me feel like more than just an athlete with a pretty face.

I lost my inhibitions. I was talkative. I had broken away from everything that had defined me in the past. And I craved more. But the lure of wrestling for Penn State kept the demon powder at bay for another year. Four years later, it began to take over.

LOOKING DOWN ON MYSELF

WHAT THE HELL HAD I done?

I was looking at the beautiful bird's-eye view picture of my final home match at Penn State as a senior, covered in the local paper.

What the hell had I done?

For the first time in my wrestling life, I had done cocaine before a match.

That's what the hell I did.

I had been doing coke for years, and had even done it before training sometimes, but until my last match, I'd always kept myself cocaine-free on the mat—kept my healthy addiction to wrestling separate from my drug addiction to cocaine. It was my church and state. The wrestling mat was my temple, where I felt the power I had since second grade. Where I didn't need drugs to get high. Now I'd broken the wall between my worlds. Ducked behind the bleachers just before they announced my name and done it.

Why?

It had nothing to do with my confidence. In fact, my confidence was peaking. I was the defending national bronze medalist, an NCAA All-American, and the first wrestler in Penn State history to win over one hundred matches. I wasn't nervous at the pre-match ceremony honoring my career. I never shied away from the spotlight on the mat. And it wasn't my opponent. He was a three-time New Jersey state champion, but I wasn't going to let him beat me.

It wasn't my lack of spiritual strength. I didn't pray before my battles, but I had learned to quiet my mind before matches, thanks to a sports psychologist who worked with us Penn State wrestlers on relaxation and visualization techniques. I pictured myself winning the fight in every position. Overrode worst-case scenarios with positive imagery. Replayed painful losses so I'd never make the same mistake twice. Made myself aware of any limitations I had: injuries, aches, pains. I heightened all of them in my mind before a match—my way of telling my body to save every ounce of power and aggression for after the whistle was blown.

It wasn't my pre-match anxiety. That was typical. I loved the stress, which helped fuel my exhilaration once the match started. Unlike the anxiety I felt as a teenager worrying about the future, I had always controlled my pre-match anxiety and used it to empower myself. I took the seeds of self-doubt and sowed them so I never got overconfident, no matter how high my opponent was ranked before we entered the ring. My anxiety kept me grounded.

That was the exact opposite of what cocaine filled me with: fear. Fear I had never felt before. Fear, not of losing, but of having no control in the one place I had felt I controlled my destiny since I was seven years old.

What the hell had I done?

I kept saying that to myself as I paced behind the bleachers like a trapped animal. There was no way out of this. I was going to be found out. The fear overwhelmed me. My heart felt like it was going to explode. I was going to be wheeled out of here on a stretcher to end my career.

What the hell had I done?

I had no explanation. There was no explanation, except that I was an addict, which I refused to admit. I had refused to let this bring me down in my battle arena. That would make me weak. That would make me vulnerable. That would make me a loser. I had refused to feel that way on the mat since I had lost and fought back tears in the third grade. Until now.

I heard my name called. I walked out to an extended standing ovation, the drugs coursing through my veins. I was sick inside but had to perform. The cheers turned into the Nittany Lion chant: *We are Penn State.*

Yes, "we." There were two people in front of the crowd right then: John the wrestler and John the addict. I had no idea which one would survive. Wrestling had been my anchor, and now my addiction was pulling it up in front of thousands of cheering fans, all celebrating me being the winningest wrestler in Penn State's storied history.

ALL-AMERICAN ADDICT

BEFORE THAT NIGHT OF my last home match, I had survived everything college, cocaine, and wrestling had thrown at me. In fact, I didn't even come in contact with cocaine my first year at Penn State. Never sought it out, despite the craving I had the summer before college started. Because I wanted something more: to be the best wrestler at Penn State.

I survived temptation when the roommate I requested, an All-American transfer from another school whom I'd met on a recruiting trip, turned out to be much crazier than I thought. He would jump me from out of the blue, lock me in a hold, and I'd have to wrestle my way out of the predicament. It could happen while walking across campus or through a building lobby. He attacked me from behind as I got ready for a date. I split my lip on the sliding closet door, leaving me with an upper lip the size of a golf ball, black thread stitching the cut all the way to my nostril, and a face no sorority girl was going to kiss. Another time he grabbed me from behind. I got my hips in position and tossed him head over heels, and he landed on his head, cracking open the skin of his skull on the tile floor. He actually began laughing and howling with pleasure as the blood flowed through his dark hair and dripped down his face. Not long after that, I began avoiding him and staying out of the dorm room as much as possible.

I survived when I started pulling the same shit I did in high school and tried to fake my way through classes. In the evenings, while everyone was studying and doing classwork, I would go over to Dan's frat house looking for something to do. It wasn't long before I learned there was no pretending being prepared at Penn State. My writing professor was the first to contact the athletic academic counselor to let her know I was falling short and would need extra work. Unlike high school, I actually listened, pulling off a string of A papers to finish strong. I even enjoyed some classes, especially my photography and marketing courses.

I had no choice but to survive. My biggest fear now was to fall short, become academically ineligible, and miss my chance to be a varsity wrestler for Penn State as a freshman. I pushed through Coach Lorenzo's grueling workouts. I became a warrior, unafraid of anyone, determined to win a spot on varsity over the three guys in front of me. I spent nights after practice with ice bags wrapped around my bruised and battered joints. I arrived early to have a trainer tape my ankle, knee, and fingers—armor protecting any part of my body that felt vulnerable.

When the time came, I tore through the first two challengers. First was a senior, a former state champion, lifeguard, frat boy, and big man on campus. I took him down and clamped him to his back so quickly and easily that he left the room, quit the team, and became captain of the cheerleading squad instead. Next up was another senior, this time a tough street-fighter type who spent his free time in a motorcycle gang. He was a scrapper—a real-life bar room brawler—who I wouldn't want to mess with outside the ring. But inside? He couldn't intimidate me even when our bout turned to a fistfight. I thumped him too.

The stage was set for my final challenge: a wrestle-off against a two-time Maryland state champ, a strong farm boy whom I had previously torn apart during my recruiting visit. He told our teammates he was confident that this was his year. I used that confidence against him to get the first takedown and then cautiously controlled the first period, waiting to see if he showed me something I had not seen before. He didn't. I took bottom position to start the second period and quickly rolled out for an escape to my feet. I immediately came back in, tying up his arm, faking one way, and exerting a Japanese arm throw in the opposite direction he was anticipating. My explosive arm throw dislocated his shoulder. The match was stopped.

I had won my spot. I made my debut in my Penn State singlet at the East Stroudsburg Collegiate Open, blazing through the bracket and winning the tournament. I made my home debut in Rec Hall just after that, against a top-ranked opponent and all-around aggressive brute from Cal Poly who was ranked fifth in the country. When we stepped out of bounds in the first round and the referee blew the whistle, I stopped but he didn't. He bulled me off the mat, across the gym floor, and up onto the scorer's table. The crowd gasped, but all I thought was, *What an asshole this guy is*. I baited him by walking meekly back to the center, my body language reading *I'm totally intimidated. Come at me again like a bull and I'll crumble*. And when he came at me like a bull again, I stood firm and allowed him to bear hug my torso. When he did, I over-locked and clamped down on his arms, stepped in between his legs, popped my hips with extreme force, and took him for a high-flying ride with me in a chest-to-chest arching Salto with a twist. I scored the feet-to-back takedown, and the match was stopped as he rolled to his back in agony. EMS rushed in. I shook his hand as he was rolled out to the hospital. It was not the way I wanted to win, but it was a legal technique, and the referee raised my arm in an upset victory over a top national contender.

I later heard that he had broken his neck, and he never competed again. I got my win, but we lost to Cal Poly, and nothing after that went the way we wanted. Our team steadily fell apart and dropped in the rankings. We lost three starters—all of them nationally ranked—due to academic ineligibility. We lost another to injury. Me? I was

41

taken down by a different foe. I contracted gladiatorum, a strain of herpes unique to wrestlers. It was all over my face and even written about in the newspaper. I was 8–0 and nationally ranked at the time. My *skin condition* cleared up, and I proceeded to go on the worst losing streak of my career.

It started at the match against Florida. Free of the virus on my face, I stayed out drinking the night before with some upperclassmen, trying to seduce a girl. I lost my match. That the coaches blamed the upperclassman didn't matter. Nothing anybody said mattered. I had lost for the first time at Penn State, and my failure stuck in my head like it hadn't since I lost in third grade. It took me five matches to break the streak and eke out a tie against a Naval Academy wrestler—a result that pulled me out of my funk and into the winning streak that led to my first NCAA National Tournament in Des Moines.

Only one other guy from the team made it, a senior named Sam, and while everyone else left for spring break, he and I trained on campus. The night before we left for Des Moines, Sam shared how happy he was to be finished with wrestling. I figured he meant going out as an All-American. *Hell no, I'll be lucky to make it past the second round. I hate wrestling.* Sam told me his father had been his coach in high school and had made him wrestle, berated him at every practice, managed every plate of food, and forced Sam to go out on after-dinner runs every evening while he followed in the car.

I didn't love that my father never supported my wrestling life, but I had never appreciated him more. I resolved never to be like either of our fathers when I became a dad. About anything. Ever. When Sam and I fell short in placing in Des Moines, he was ecstatic; I was devastated. But then *Amateur Wrestling News* named me as the top freshman in the country at my weight class. My mindset shifted. I was more determined than ever to become a national champion, and I had a new goal too: the 1980 Olympic Trials.

Dan and I had been picked to compete for the New York Athletic Club, or NYAC, which was the top Olympic wrestling club in the nation. At my first national event with the NYAC, I won, defeating the top NYAC guy and solidifying my spot on the club. If that wasn't enough, Dan Gable's wrestling camp in Pittsburgh hired me as their only college-age clinician. My wrestling hero and gold medalist from the 1972 Olympics—the guy I begged to do takedowns with four years earlier—now wrestled with me *for real* between our teaching sessions.

As I headed back to Virginia for the summer after camp, everything was about as perfect as it could be. I took a job working construction for a high school buddy, who had become a bit of a DC gangster and hired former wrestlers to roll into bad sections of DC and tear apart buildings.

Yep, everything was perfect…until I learned my friend dabbled in more than construction. He also moved large quantities of cocaine to local dealers.

Rather than run away from the source, I ran right into it. Almost a year to the day since first trying cocaine, I was all in. With no wrestling, I had no reason to stop. By the end of the summer, I was basically paid with a Ziploc bag filled with white powder, which I snorted all weekend to get that full feeling I had been longing for.

◆◆◆

WHEN I RETURNED TO Penn State, I steered clear of cocaine as I worked to keep my grades up and be ready for wrestling season. Not that I had any money for cocaine on campus…or money for anything. NCAA rules did not allow any funding to go toward things like film or art supplies, and also did not allow a scholarship athlete to have an on-campus job. We made some money off-book during football season selling programs at Beaver Stadium, but I basically lived off of boxed mac and cheese. As the season progressed, I started feeling sorry for myself and alone, thinking no one understood how brutal and difficult my life was while I was living off $100 a month—not nearly enough to feed myself properly after hours of daily training.

It got worse. That fall, I got a call that my cousin Susan, just a few years younger than me, had been paralyzed in a car accident with three other girls riding home from a football game. She was sitting in the back of the car and wasn't wearing her seatbelt when they hit a drainage ditch. Her spine just snapped. She was the only one injured.

Susan and I were close, and I went back to DC to see her in the hospital. What I saw made me freeze. Her bed was a table that got flipped every hour so she didn't get bedsores. There was a halo screwed into her temples and attached to a cable on two weighted pulleys, designed to gently get everything flowing in her back so the nerves would hopefully start working again.

I did everything I could to keep her spirits up. If her table was turned down, I rolled underneath to talk to her face to face. Who was I to complain about being on the floor, when I couldn't comprehend what she was going through, and what she'd have to go through just to try and regain use of her fingers? I had broken someone's neck less than a year before. I always knew there was a risk to my sport. But this shook me. I realized just how much life could change in an instant.

Susan eventually did more than regain the use of her fingers. She moved her arms too. She persevered. She used a motorized recumbent to exercise her legs, to keep them strong even when they couldn't move on their own. Years later, she walked down the aisle at her sister's wedding with a specialized walker that moved her legs forward. It was incredible. Everybody in the church was in tears, because everybody knew Susan's story.

No one knew me—not even me. If I was really the man I believed I was, I would have straightened up my situation. Stopped drinking. Stopped doing drugs. I saw Susan's pain. I felt it. I felt it just as I had years before, when I wrestled in Poland as a junior national champion. Not wanting to leave as the Ugly Americans on our final night, the team gathered up all of our remaining złoty, placed the crumbled bills and coins in a paper bag, and went down to the town square. We found a man who had lost a leg sitting beside a fountain.

We all sat and knelt around him and presented him with the bag. He stared at us with tears in his eyes, and as we left, each of us shook his hand. But did I go back home that summer and realize how fragile life is and change? No. It was summer—time to drink and smoke and enjoy my All-American life and become the All-American athlete I longed to be. And then a different kind of Ugly American: the full-blown addict who destroyed it all.

After I saw Susan, I made sure I wore my seatbelt and stopped throwing myself a pity party. I returned to school, recommitted myself to dominating my opponents, qualified for the NCAA Nationals, and suffered a heartbreaking first-round loss to an opponent I had defeated earlier in the season.

Deflated, my coach told me to not hit the bars like most disappointed wrestlers, but to sit in the arena and watch the champs. Learn how they carry themselves through each match and onto the podium. Know what you don't know and then make it happen. It was literally and figuratively the most sobering experience of my life. That, and maybe Susan's perseverance had taught me something. By the time I got to the Olympic Trials in Madison, Wisconsin, I was ready.

Problem was, my country was not. No one left those trials to wrestle for gold. The United States led sixty-five countries in a boycott of the 1980 Summer Olympics in Moscow, protesting the Soviet Union's invasion of Afghanistan. My only consolation prize was that I qualified for the twenty-and-under Junior World Team run by the US Olympic coach. His camp demanded ten miles of running a day, along with two hours of live wrestling sessions, where I battled the legendary Dave Schultz, of Foxcatcher fame, and his brother Mark for the first time. They took me every match but also sharpened my resolve, and I left camp a better wrestler.

Problem was, that meant I was also going home to be a better addict. I took the job at the construction company again, and again took my paychecks in Ziploc bags.

❖❖❖

WHEN I RETURNED TO campus junior year, I was once again able to control my addiction when it came to my matches. But for the first time, I brought some cocaine back to campus and got high before a few preseason workouts. When the cocaine ran out, I was too broke to find more. I had used all I had left of my summer "paychecks." Wrestling once again became my sole addiction, and I was on a mission to place at nationals, if I could survive all the other stupid shit I did to get high.

My campaign started ominously, but not because of any drugs: I was a man behind a literal mask. A road trip back to DC with a bunch of my teammates turned into a weekend of raucous Georgetown nightlife and after-hours street fights. One fight had left me with a knife wound in my left thigh, my face scraped, my nose broken by the concrete sidewalk, and all of us running from the police. We made it back to my family's basement, where my sister Teri, now an ER nurse, made me go to the hospital. They stitched up my leg and told me to get an ENT doctor to set my broken nose. I couldn't be bothered. I let it set as it was so I could get back to the wrestling room Monday. Which is how I ended up wearing a protective mask the first tournament of the season. I cruised to the finals where I faced Jeff Parker who had dominated his way through the brackets. Between rounds Parker would strut around the arena in his flashy purple-and-gold LSU attire accessorized with a flamboyant tasseled hat. Parker was extremely strong, he locked me up around the neck; I was disoriented wearing the mask. I got thrown to the mat in a tight headlock and lost 10–5. At least the crowd couldn't see my humiliated face as Parker celebrated his victory. I threw it away after that match, my broken nose slowly healed, and I stayed motivated to finding a way to beat an opponent as fierce as Parker. I was hungry to win and also just plain hungry, because I was still broke. I was even desperate enough to steal to feed myself.

I had just returned from a prestigious tournament in Chicago during winter break after another crazy but much closer loss to Parker, and State College was deserted. I was hungry, no one was around, and I only had enough money to buy a loaf of bread. I grabbed the bread and a piece of cheese, and then headed to the cashier with my gloves and the cheese in one hand and the loaf of bread in the other. I put the loaf on the counter and paid for it while trying to hide the cheese in my gloves, but the clerk busted me as I left. I considered making an easy dash for the door as he came around the counter, but at that exact moment I saw Coach Lorenzo through the store window, walking down the sidewalk with a recruit and his parents. I ducked back as they passed and decided to bring shame only on myself. I surrendered, and luckily the story was kept out of the news.

My near-arrest shook me enough to focus on training for the NCAA tournament. My intense training, pushing myself to a never-before-reached threshold, left me in tears. My tears turned to laughter when I realized I had broken through to a new level. I worked harder than I ever had, and I knew as our contingent of four Lions headed to nationals that I was going to place. I was not going to lose a match that I deserved to win.

My body's lactic acids were burning, draining my power and performance, as they often did in the first round of a tournament, but I shook off that usual slow start and won my first match. In fact, the entire Penn State contingent swept round one and was in third place in the team category. But there was little time for celebration. Up next in my bracket: Parker, who had demolished his first-round opponent and stared me down confidently as I stepped on to the mat.

I knew I needed a new strategy, so I hit him like a freight train, with my head in his gut, and plowed through on an explosive double-leg takedown. I rode and turned him on his back several times; he never had a chance to recover. I got the win, but also got a deep bloody gash on my chin. The gash was stitched up that night but it didn't stop me from stitching together another dominating win the next day over the defending national champ before losing in the semifinals to one of Dan Gable's guys from Iowa. Dan knew I liked to take that initial shot, so he just had his guy sit back and catch me when I did. I lunged in right off the whistle, hitting my blast double—a modified version of my "patented" second-grade football tackle—but he under-hooked my arms as I wrapped his legs and pancaked me, like a flapjack being flipped on a hot skillet. I spent the next two minutes fighting off my back until I couldn't anymore.

Undaunted, I wanted to show Coach Lorenzo I had learned my lesson watching the champs last year and vowed to come back and take third. I did by coming back through the consolation brackets and beating Iowa State's national runner-up Perry Hummel. I then watched Dan's guy get upset by Oklahoma's future Olympic champion, Mark Schultz, in the final. Mark became the national champion. As I took my third-place spot next to him on the podium, I looked up at him and had only one thing to say: *Hey, I have some weed. You want to smoke?* We ended up in a squash court, breaking up the bud and cleaning the seeds on the copy of the winner's bracket they gave him. *Amateur Wrestling News* voted mine the best performance.

If they only knew just how true that was, in ways nobody could see yet.

◆◆◆

I RETURNED TO CAMPUS for the end of my junior year one of the top wrestlers in the country and a genuine campus celebrity. To the victor goes the spoils: I started dating the most popular girl on campus. My notoriety grew as I took down Penn State's number-one recruit at the Eastern Freestyle tournament held at Rec Hall. He was a local hero who was not only the top-ranked high school wrestler in the nation at my weight class, but also the top recruit in the nation period. A kid who was a big fan of that recruit came over afterward to compliment me on the beating and say how he was glad some of the wind was taken out of his friend's sails, because his head was getting too big.

When our recruit arrived on campus that fall, he did not challenge me at my weight class. Instead, he cut down and dropped a weight class, in which he also became an All-American. We even became good friends. Because that's what wrestling does. It humbles you…just not enough for me when it came to cocaine, which now filled most of my non-match days. My girlfriend and I made quite the striking couple, and we met a guy that controlled all of the drug traffic in Happy Valley. He threw parties in his opulent homes and liked to be around beautiful women. He loaded me with cocaine so we'd grace him with our presence. I was happy to oblige.

But while I now had a source for cocaine, I was even more determined to make it to the top of the NCAA podium in my final college season. That summer, before my senior year, I often woke up in the middle of the night replaying the moment I got pinned in the semifinals. I was so close and knew I could get all the way to the top. I vowed to get stronger, and took a summer job with my sister's boyfriend, who had a large DC-area landscaping company. I mowed steep hills at apartment complexes, tying a rope to the back of the mower and then lowering and pulling it up with my feet planted in a wrestling stance. As I shuffled along each hill, I imitated pulling a leg attack on my opponent—never relenting, or else I would slip under the mower blades and cut myself up.

I got stronger every day, pushing my physical limits in the humid DC heat. But I was also getting weaker. I was still working for the construction company for my bags of coke. Plus, it wasn't just the cocaine that threatened my life that summer. One hot night, driving out of DC, I got arrested for drunk driving on the George Washington Parkway and thrown into lockup at Washington National Airport. I was released the next day and ended up with reduced charges after I faced the court and admitted I had five or six drinks. Apparently everyone who came before that judge lied about his or her drunken state, and he took the opportunity with me to lecture the court. *This young man is the first ever to come in front of me and say anything other than he had one or two drinks. What do people take me for, a fool? I'm so sick and tired of hearing, "One or two, Your Honor."*

My candid response coupled with my otherwise clean driving record led to his leniency. But did my honesty with the judge make me honest with myself about how far gone I was? No. My addiction was pushing its way into everything I loved and pushing me further and further from the truth and honesty I had been raised to honor. I was living a lie, testing the limits of my God-given talents, and my body, and now my life.

Then, I pushed even farther. That summer, I injected cocaine for the first time in a sort of blood brother ritual with a friend. We knew it was dangerous, but that didn't stop us. We agreed before inserting the needle that if one of us died and the other one lived, that person should take the body and put it up by the creek that separated our neighborhoods and not tell anybody. No one should get blamed.

We never discussed what would happen if we both died.

We lived, and I went back to Penn State my senior year with dreams of winning my first NCAA title and a big bag of cocaine in my duffel. No more needles, though—as if that was some kind of moral victory and meant things weren't falling apart. Which they were. The first sign was that I returned to campus senior year without having lined up a place to live, like every other student had done. I ended up living out of my Honda Civic for the first weeks of the semester, crashing wherever I could, and using the team's locker room at Rec Hall to shower.

I managed to get clean before the season, which started with high expectations, as I was ranked second in the country behind Dave Schultz. I had only wrestled with Schultz as a junior, but even then he was clearly one of the very best in the entire world. We finally met in a dual meet in Tulsa, Oklahoma, and prior to the match, I found myself nervous in an unfamiliar way. I had seen Dave perform and realized his potential to put me in situations I had never visualized. Dave was dangerous. Sure, I had broken someone's neck, but Dave had the power to paralyze an opponent with his explosive technique and unique positioning. I thought about Susan. I wondered if that could be me, but then I fell back into my pre-match ritual of turning my anxiety into fuel.

Our battle began. I took the first shot on Dave with an explosive deep single leg, but Dave was able to get around my neck and tighten the head and arm lock like a boa constrictor, cutting off the blood supply to my brain. *Let go of the leg or go unconscious* was what his hold told me, but I came up with another option and, with my last moment of pre-suffocation consciousness, tried to drive us out of bounds. The ref, who had no idea I was being strangled, blew the whistle and stopped the action. Able to breathe again, I attacked with a different approach—a head in the gut double—that scored the first takedown on Schultz that season. But with Schultz in top position in the second period, I got stuck on my back in one of his patented spine-breaking leg rides. I submitted and turned to my back. Done.

I met Schultz one more time before the national tournament started, at the East-West All-Star event where I represented the East. He beat me again and opened a deep cut around my eye socket in the process. I got stitched up at the arena and upped my determination to beat him at nationals.

I returned to Penn State as a man on a mission. No one was going to beat my work ethic. I had never missed a practice, a match, or ever lost a challenge match since taking that varsity spot at the beginning of my Penn State career, and I wasn't about to start now. I would lead by example and groom the next generation to take my place—but they would have to fight for the right. Every day, I walked into the wrestling room with the intent of not only breaking my opponents, but also protecting myself in the process. I figured the only way a challenger could take me out would be by injuring me during practice.

Which did happen. One of the underclassmen had thrust his hand toward my face as we battled, and his finger knifed deeply into my eye socket, cutting the white of my eye. I fell to the mat clutching my face and screaming obscenities. The trainer pulled my hands away and wrapped the eye, which was bleeding from the socket, and got me to the hospital. Coach met me at the hospital. With my eye patched up, the doc said I would be fine, but we were only concerned about one thing: could I wrestle? We faced Lehigh University the next day. Doc said I could, and I did. And I won.

There would be no excuses for losing in this part of my life—no lies, no blame. After letting my pre-match anxiety wash over me, I walked into every match fueled with confidence, regardless of who was on the other side—even Schultz. I had doubled down on wrestling again. My addiction could never break through here.

Until it did. The night of my last home match.

WINNER & LOSER

I STOOD IN FRONT of thousands of cheering fans, the opposing team, referees, my coaches, and my team, high on the cocaine I did beneath the bleachers where everyone was standing for me now.

Can they tell? Do they know I am unworthy of their praise right now?

I felt weak as I walked onto the mat. I was tentative, thinking my heart was exploding. As the match began, the crowd, given nothing to cheer about and sensing I was off, had grown silent, which only made me more aware of the sound of my racing heart. Well into the second period, I was still thinking I was going to collapse, EMTs would whisk me to the ER, doctors would order blood tests, and all would be revealed. The newspapers that had covered my success would relish the chance to document my fall: *John Hanrahan, Penn State's winningest wrestler, collapsed on the mat last night after the university paid tribute to him. He was found to have cocaine in his system.*

What the hell had I done?

I had to shake it off. I had to. I had made a mistake that I could not undo, but the addiction would only score a point tonight, not win the match. This was not the night that my house of cards would collapse, revealing my addiction and my double life. The conference

53

tournament was next week, and I would not make the same mistake again. Ever again. *Ever.*

I took my opponent down, turned him on his back, and finally felt at ease, winning 11–1, a major decision covered by the local paper. At the conclusion of the event, they brought me to center mat again and presented me with the Ridge Riley Outstanding Wrestler Award.

As I looked at that story the next morning, just three days shy of my twenty-second birthday, I resolved to stay clean. I still had the control to keep myself pure for the rest of the season, and I blazed through the conference tournament, winning it once again. I then went into two weeks of intensive training for my final NCAA Nationals. My sense of mission recovered, I rolled past my first test in the NCAA tournament against a dirty head-butting wrestler from Nebraska I had lost to earlier that year. I then took a hard-fought battle against a guy from Old Dominion in match two.

Things were going as planned as day one concluded, and I rested up for the quarterfinals. The following morning, I found myself flying through the air with my opponent from Navy. As our combined weight hit the mat, the point of total impact was my right thumb. It snapped. I had never felt such pain. My body was ringing with it.

This was not how it was supposed to be. This was not how champs went down. This was not how I went out. I refused to stop. I fell behind in the score and vowed between periods that I would never get my thumb fixed if I was unable to come back and win this bout.

Use the thumb, Hanrahan. You're down by five points, and if you don't come back and win this match, you can never get this fixed.

I lost.

But I refused to bow out. The second day at the NCAAs is known as "The Blood Round," because that's what you see as everyone fights tooth and nail to survive. Anyone left standing after The Blood Round earns a chance to wrestle on day three, a guaranteed place on the podium, and coveted NCAA All-American status. I stayed in despite my immobilized thumb and limited use of my right hand.

I took out my next opponent from Wisconsin and then beat one of Dan Gable's guys from Iowa, earning my spot in day three. I lost a tough one to an All-American from New Mexico, but came back to beat an opponent from Yale to finish my college career with a win, fifth place on the podium, and All-American status once again.

As I climbed the podium, I heard the announcer introduce me as completing my collegiate career with the Most Wins in Penn State's history with 105 wins.

But I was disappointed—both that I never got to face Schultz in the finals, and that I would never be enshrined in Rec Hall at Penn State as a National Champion. I would never be one of the exalted few—big pictures of the biggest stars that ring the top of the wrestling complex walls. Every time I entered the Hall from that day forward, I would be reminded of my failure. Mine is one of the commemorative plaques beneath them, celebrating Penn State All-Americans over a century of wrestling.

But I was more than disappointed. I was over. My four years competing for Penn State were done. The next Olympics were two years away. There was no going back. No undoing past mistakes and avenging past losses. No daily anchor of wrestling to keep the drugs away.

Wrestling gave me more than just a sense of power and control. From second grade on, it had given me the approval that I never got anywhere else. I hid my drug use from people, not only because I did not want to taint the sport I loved, but because I couldn't bear to taint what others thought of me.

If I was addicted to anything besides wrestling and drugs, it was the praise. I wanted people to see me as the best and strongest version of myself—the winner I usually was, even in defeat. Wrestling was my stage. At the end of every performance, there was a judgment—from the referee, but also everyone else. I didn't and still don't know why I did cocaine before my last match at Penn State. But I do know the reason for my self-imposed panic attack: I would be exposed as a fraud to everyone. I would wonder what they thought of me, like I always did, but this time I would be exposed as an addict unworthy of their praise and applause.

Now what? I loved and still longed for the feeling I got on the mat and for the high I got from cocaine. In my last match, drugs and wrestling had come together. Where did that leave me?

The terrible answer came the summer my collegiate career ended, when I freebased cocaine for the first time with a few friends holed up in a seedy DC apartment. The drug sped through my body. It overtook me. I crawled into the bathroom. My ears were ringing. I splashed cold water on my face, and the *sound* of the water made my ears hurt. I threw up. I wound up awake for days, looking for more, and when there was none, I crawled around on the floor, fishing around in the shag carpet, picking at every little white piece and hoping it would burn like a rock of cocaine.

I never got my thumb fixed, nor anything else in my life that was broken. I was crawling around on the floor looking for rock because *I* was broken. I was making more money than I ever had in my life and was sure nothing would be the same again. I was right in more ways than one.

MODEL BEHAVIOR

AFTER I MADE THE team my freshman year, Coach sent me down to Mac's Haberdashery in Happy Valley to get fitted for my varsity blazer. The morning I was there, a photographer snapped shots of a Penn State sweater Mac was advertising in the *Daily Collegian*. Mac looked at me and said, *Hey, you're a good-lookin' fella. Will you do me a favor and try this on?* I'd never posed for a picture outside of school, but reluctantly said okay. I was too shy to say no. Mac found me a sweater in my size and we headed outside the shop on College Avenue, where the photographer took shots as I leaned against a tree. The next day at practice, the full-page ad was up in the wrestling room: "The Look is Penn State," with a picture of me in the sweater, smiling.

My debut as a fashion model. I also thought it would be my finale. I was wrong. Just when I was leaving the wrestling stage, the book of my life opened to the modeling page.

The night my eye was cut by the underclassman that knifed his finger into my eye socket, I was worried I would miss my next match at Lehigh's Stabler Arena in Allentown. Thankfully, the doctor at the hospital cleared me, excusing me from my test that morning and sending me on my way with an eye patch and a *Go beat Lehigh*! My match was an uneventful, 17–4 thrashing of my opponent.

Meanwhile, one hundred miles away in New York City, it was the beginning of something more eventful than I could possibly imagine. Our match was televised. A guy named Scott Copeland happened to be smoking a joint and looking for something to watch on TV, when he stopped on the broadcast just as I was about to start wrestling and my name appeared on screen: *John Hanrahan, Falls Church, Virginia.*

Scott immediately picked up the phone, called directory assistance, got my parents' number, and spoke with my father, who put him in touch with me. He told me I jumped off the screen, but not for my wrestling skills. He knew little about wrestling. He was a fashion agent in New York City who had discovered several top models and wanted to represent me. Something about me just stood out.

Honestly, I figured he was a pervert. A lot of athletes got calls for "modeling," which turned out to be propositions for sleazy soft-core porn magazines like *Blueboy*. It sounded crazy that a wrestler with a broken nose and a face that had been sewn back together in eight different places would attract the attention of anyone working in high fashion. Then I looked up the guys he said he discovered and represented—guys on the cover of *GQ*, and even the face of the hot new Calvin Klein campaign. He was the real deal.

I called Scott back, and he asked when I could come to New York City. His instincts were right about my looks. Everyone liked that I wasn't just another cookie-cutter model. He said he'd shown Bruce Weber the pictures I had sent up, and Bruce wanted to shoot me as a wrestler for *L'Uomo Vogue. This never happens,* Scott kept saying over and over. Then he told me what the job paid, although I would have taken anything. I was broke.

What, I get paid that much? I'm ready now!

On my first trip to New York City, I didn't just shoot with Bruce. I met with Giorgio Armani, received an invite from Calvin Klein to attend his daughter's Sweet Sixteen at Studio 54, and was soon working with other renowned photographers like Francesco Scavullo. But Bruce was the first to book me. Despite it being my first shoot, I wasn't nervous at all. The nervous kid who posed outside Mac's that day was gone. I treated the shoot like a match and arrived on set with the same confidence I brought into the ring. But it was more than that. I had enjoyed studying photography at Penn State, and I was fascinated by the whole process. I was amazed that my first experience on the other side of the camera was with a guy who had changed the whole fashion industry with his work for Calvin Klein. I looked at the camera like I was looking at the most beautiful girl I could imagine. He told me that there were too many handsome guys who were just flat in pictures, which was why he booked inexperienced guys like surfers and athletes for big campaigns, like the pole-vaulter he used in a Calvin Klein ad. He liked real men who had more behind their eyes. Guys who could kick your ass, take your girl, and make her love them.

Bruce discovered what I had inside and outside and captured it with his camera. He would tell me to put something on to see how it felt and just move around naturally—then suddenly say, *Stop! That's perfect. Just tilt your head a little bit this way. Eyes over here, eyes over there. You look so handsome. Oh hold that…that's beautiful, Johnny.*

Afterward, Bruce took the time to answer my technical questions for the high-level photography classwork I had to complete. I grilled him about the Ansel Adams zone system, calculations for developing film, and the different shades of gray the same way I drilled Dan Gable about wrestling techniques. Bruce said it sounded like I knew more about some of those things than he did. As I got ready to head back to campus, exhilarated by the idea of these shots appearing in Italian *Vogue*, Bruce left me with one piece of advice about the modeling business: Don't give up everything and focus solely on modeling. There's a lot of creepy people in this business; keep doing your wrestling too. I said I would.

I spent the next year of my life driving back and forth from campus to Manhattan in my battered Honda Civic, each job seemingly bigger than the last. Bruce, Scavullo, and Juan Ramos shot me for *Vogue*. I had the cover of *Menswear* shot by Albert Bray. I was featured in Macy's runway show at the Waldorf Astoria—all before moving to New York and making any real effort to pursue that line of work. Initially, I only knew how big the jobs were because I was making good money—which allowed me to buy drugs *and* food—and because my college girlfriend was jealous. She wanted to be a model, was on the cover of the Women of Penn State calendar and hot rod auto magazines. She begged to attend shoots with me, hoping to get discovered. Then the magazine ads and editorials I had shot started turning up on newsstands, and my agent let me know I had compiled a portfolio of work, or "tear sheets," that would enable me to work in any fashion market in the world.

My girlfriend thought I was crazy not to move to New York City and travel the world. But all I wanted to do was keep wrestling. Not because it kept my addiction to cocaine at bay, but because I longed to be on that stage again. Modeling just didn't do it for me the way wrestling did. I would never be an NCAA champion, but I still had three dreams on the table: to wear the USA singlet as an adult and to be an Olympic and World Champion, now that I had graduated from the Penn State wrestling stage.

Well, almost graduated. I had fallen a few credits short after my senior year, but that was fine. Coach Lorenzo let me know after I signed my letter of intent that my scholarship was for five years, all expenses paid. One reason for this was that it gave me the option of "redshirting" as a freshman athlete, sitting out a year and becoming more physically mature and seasoned without losing a year of eligibility. But I opted to compete my first four years straight through, leaving time for completing my coursework on the back end. Five-year scholarships gave guys like me who struggled with the demands of being student athletes a chance to finish their degrees, something that was very important to Coach. We called him Papa Bear, part father figure but mostly part bear. Papa Bear kept me on the team as a grad assistant wrestling coach. He had no idea I was an addict.

Still, with cocaine now seeping into all parts of Penn State and Happy Valley life, money in my pocket from the modeling gigs, and me no longer wrestling for the school, I was less concerned with appearances. I found myself doing cocaine to fill the void between wrestling opportunities. Doing it made me feel not just high, but really cool.

Then, the winter of my fifth year at Penn State, something happened to suppress my addiction: I climbed back onto the wrestling stage to realize the first of my dreams.

WRESTLING WITH THE FUTURE

I HAD JUST TURNED twenty-three when I learned I would represent the United States against the Soviet Union, the team dominating world competition. Coach Lorenzo gave me the news that the US Wrestling Federation chose me just a few days before the competition. He had confidence that I was ready. He knew I had been training for the 1984 Olympic Trials. He just didn't know that it was wrestling legend Rick Sanders-style training: workout then drink, drugs, and party, sometimes at the same time. I took those few days and the car ride with Coach across the frozen Pennsylvania interstate to sober up and think about my opponent: Yuri Vorobiev, the current world silver medalist. We would meet at Stabler Arena, the same one where my agent had seen me wrestling, and the site of my bloody loss against Dave Schultz in the East-West All-Star Meet. Powerful moments in my life. I had no doubt this would be a third, for better or worse.

We arrived at the USA locker room, and New York Athletic Club chairman Sonny Greenhalgh greeted me first. I was sure Sonny had a lot to do with me getting chosen for this event. His club was the reigning national club champ; since my freshman year, they had sponsored me to compete for them when the college season ended. I then moved to shake hands with Team USA Coach Stan Dziedzic, who had been the world champ at my weight in 1977 and recruited me as I was coming out of high school, when he was the Michigan State assistant coach. Coach handed me my first USA adult warm-ups, and beneath them, I saw it. The first part of my dream realized: a brand-new, bright blue singlet with red and white trim and the USA emblem across the chest.

After greeting my teammates, who came from all over the country and only a couple of whom I knew, I retreated to my locker to change. I was nervous, but I felt relaxed too, and as I pulled on my USA singlet for the first time, I was only thinking about one thing: wearing a different shoe on each foot. I had a blue and white pair and a red and white pair. I put red and white on the right foot and blue and white on the left foot. I'd never seen anyone do that before.

I taped up the areas of my body that felt weak, including my broken thumb that had cost me a chance to face Schultz again. I then taped my other thumb so that Vorobiev wouldn't hone in on it as a weak spot, as the Soviets are notorious for snapping fingers and targeting injured areas. I usually taped up my right knee for stability—the years of pounding had left it with floating pieces the doctor called gravel—but tonight the tape didn't feel right. I was used to having our Penn State trainer do his artful wrap, and mine felt restrictive. So I cut it off and just pulled up a kneepad for protection.

How far I had come since the days when I didn't even have kneepads: sixteen years since I started wrestling, a decade since I was a junior champion in Poland, and now, a chance to win the approval of my country on my home soil.

Team USA jogged together, single file, onto the floor to warm up in front of the packed house. By then, I was used to crowds this big or bigger. It was the Soviets that captured my attention. I had only seen them up close once, the last time I saw Coach Stan Dziedzic: on my hotel floor when I visited Michigan State as a high school senior. I had studied them though, and knew what I was up against. Midsections like steel cages—not just strong abs, but gnarly points protruding like spikes out of their rib cages, like the bones had adapted to extreme stress over the years of grinding and grappling. Now, I was just feet away from those muscles beneath their warm-up jackets, red with CCCP in white letters across the chest, and minutes away from facing one of their best.

I spotted Vorobiev. My excitement turned to nervousness, filling me with my usual anxiety about the opportunity to go three, three-minute periods against the man. *Does anyone expect me to last past the first round?* Though Dave Schultz was, in my eyes, the best in the world, another American, Lee Kemp, held the past three world titles, having beat Vorobiev 1–0 last year. No one had beaten him since.

After warm-ups, we headed back to our locker room, where Coach gave us a nice "leave it all on the mat" motivational talk. Then we were each given a box, which contained a gift for our Soviet counterpart. We marched back to the mat and lined up across from the Soviets in our weight class. As each weight class and athlete was introduced, we walked to center mat, shook hands, and exchanged gifts.

When my name was called, I walked to center mat and shook hands with Vorobiev. I was beyond nervous by this point. There was an unusually large number of photographers mat side, and I locked eyes with one of them as I returned with my gift. It was my photojournalism teacher back at Penn State, who worked on assignment for the Associated Press. All I could think was that I hadn't turned in my assignment that had been due yesterday. Maybe she'd give me a pass without a late penalty, after seeing what I was about to go through.

The teams stood for both anthems, and the lightweights took the mat. I peeked in the box with my USSR gift: a colorful ceramic trinket with Russian letters on it. I threw it in my USA gear bag and looked up just in time to see our little guy get his arm almost ripped off in a vicious flying mare throw. As the Soviet's arm was raised in victory, I marveled how he, like all their guys, looked so much more mature and seasoned than we did. Because they were—we were amateurs competing against, in essence, professional athletes. Men who did

64

this for a better living in a country where sport and military strength were king. I had learned about and experienced this government-supported athletic machine when I competed in Poland on the USA junior team, but this was an entirely different level. The top level.

Dad was here. My dad had never been a gung-ho sports guy, and was unable to attend most of my events. But Dad was also a staunch anti-communist, a naval commander, and a top-secret weaponry scientist. He'd been in the Cold War fight for decades, and he wasn't going to miss his son taking on the Soviets. I felt him and my mom praying for my protection first and my success as a wrestler second. It comforted me that when I needed support, they could still show up, even if my dad dismissed sports in general. He loved his country. He loved his son even more.

After four more matches, I was up. We were losing the team score 2–4, and I knew a loss in my match meant no worse than a tie for the Soviets. I let the last nerves wash over me as always. My fear as I stepped onto the mat was not that I would get hurt, but that I wouldn't have enough gas and technical ability to go the distance. I told myself this guy probably smoked cigarettes and drank vodka all the time, like I had seen the Soviet team do at the Lansing hotel, the night they beat the USA team at Michigan State.

As our names were announced, Vorobiev and I walked forward and shook the judge's hand. I looked at the hammer and sickle emblem on his well-worn red singlet and felt young in my brand-new, bright blue one. Vorobiev and I then shook each other's hands and waited, eye to eye, toe to toe. For a moment I thought, *What am I doing here with this guy?* Then I realized I wasn't scared of him. I had confidence that my lungs, my array of techniques, and my tenacity were prepared to go the distance. I just had to keep myself from making a rookie mistake and getting humiliated.

Then the whistle blew, and all my nervousness, anxiety, and heightened pre-match aches and pains transformed into an energy that threw my body forward.

First Period

VOROBIEV WAS IMMEDIATELY A step ahead of me. He leached himself around my exposed arm and boom—thrust his body into an arm throw that put me in the air. I hit the mat, exposing my back. I fought not to get pinned, but already I'm down 0–3. Face to face now, I reached out sloppily, and he cleared my arm and snatched my lead leg, dropping me to the mat. I bellied down to protect myself from getting turned, and he transitioned into a lock between my thighs that jacked my hips high. He knew that if I didn't turn toward my back, the pressure would break it. I relented, and he exposed my back and scored again. 0–6. I got back to my feet, and with only a few seconds left in the period, I took a shot on him. It was a halfhearted effort, and Vorobiev stuffed my head, breaking my core posture, and came around for a takedown before the buzzer. 0–7.

I headed to my corner, feeling stupid. *I'm giving this guy way too much credit. He's strong, but not superhuman. I deserve to be in there against him. I need to get out of my head and have fun.* I told my coaches that I was going to go out and wrestle hard, the same way I did when I first discovered the sport in second grade.

Second Period

THIS TIME I CAME out aggressively. I reached and snapped Vorobiev's head. He reached, and I posted arms as I lowered my level and drove in for the hard charging football tackle I was so good at. Upon impact, I stuck my head in his gut and felt his breath get knocked out of him as I drove him to his back for a takedown plus back exposure. The satisfaction of the takedown renewed my confidence. 3–7.

As we came forehead to forehead again, I cuffed the back of his skull with my right hand, driving my left arm into a deep under hook and baiting him to pull his head exactly the way I wanted him to. He took the bait, and I stepped my hips in and unleashed a full flying headlock, taking him to his back with a thump. 5–7. But I let my guard down, and Vorobiev's savvy gained a reversal, exposing my back before the buzzer. 5–9. Still, heading to my corner, I was feeling good. My coaches were beaming. The crowd was back into it. I was having fun, and there was no place in the world I'd rather be. I had the momentum, and I knew I had the tenacity to drive this guy off the mat in the final period.

Third Period

VOROBIEV BACKPEDALED AS I drove forward. He was playing the edge and received a caution from the mat judge. I could tell he was breathing heavy; I thought about the Soviet wrestlers I saw smoking cigarettes in the hotel at Michigan State. I kept after him, and he clearly avoided engaging me. When you're not getting enough oxygen to keep up with the demands of this sport, it will suffocate and bury you. I could see that in him. I waited for my moment and finally caught him reaching, I knocked his arms out of the way, giving myself a clear path to slide into a leg attack. I knocked him back onto his hips and immediately moved up to his torso to expose his back. 8–9. Twenty-eight seconds to go. The look on his face was annoyed and slightly panicked. I had no time to waste. I got to an under-hook, not real deep, but I had to throw now to give myself the win. I brought my hips in for the same headlock throw that worked in the second period. I pulled forward with my lock around his neck and arm and popped my hips into his torso. I grabbed his head, wet and slippery with sweat, and started my throw, but halfway through his head slipped out of my lock, and I fell to the mat with no points.

Time ran out. Vorobiev escaped with a 9–8 victory.

I shook his hand and watched as his arm was raised, disappointed but keeping my head high. I shook hands with Vorobiev's coach, too. Their respect was little consolation, just like the acknowledgement and appreciation of my teammates. I knew we were now only capable of a tie if we swept the remaining three bouts. I'd let them down. I tried to console myself by remembering that I'd always grown better after a loss by going back to work and committing myself to not repeating the same mistakes. I deserved to be on the mat with Vorobiev and knew I'd get him if I ever got the chance again. Maybe I was getting closer to making my world championship dream a reality.

I headed back to Penn State less dejected, but restless. I was still dating the girl on the cover of the Women of Penn State calendar, and everyone thought we'd get married. Except me. I couldn't wait to finish up my final semester and move to New York City, where I planned on competing with the New York Athletic Club, and training for the 1984 Olympic Trials. I'd also be working with my agent, who desperately wanted me in the City full time to do high-paying commercial and print ad work.

All I wanted to do was meet girls and party to fill the space until I could wrestle again. Which turned out to be sooner than I thought. I got word that, based on my match against Vorobiev, I was chosen with three others—including Lee Kemp and Dave Schultz—to compete for a spot on the USA World Cup Team at a two-day trial tournament in Michigan. Vorobiev might have been the world silver medalist, but Kemp was gold and Schultz was golden. They were the two best wrestlers in the world at my weight, the most competitive weight class in the world. If I could build on where I left off against Vorobiev and beat them, a climb to the top of the world podium would be in my sights.

I put all decisions on hold, resisting the temptation to party too much. I flew to Michigan, fully focused on beating Kemp and Schultz.

At weigh-in the following morning, Schultz approached me and complimented my animalistic double leg against Vorobiev. He told me they watched film of the meet, and I had crushed him twice with that. Then he smiled and said, *Hey, I also saw you on the cover of a magazine, you better watch your face this weekend.* He walked away laughing. Head games!

My first match was against Kemp, built like Superman with the reflexes of a cat. I lost by two points. Lee controlled the entire match, never exposing himself to my attack, scoring when he needed to and allowing no vulnerable positions. He did the same thing to beat Vorobiev. After the match, he and I did our backroom workout to make weight for day two. We traded all kinds of positions and dimensions as we wrestled—all the drama and action that was missing from the mat that day. At that moment, I learned from Kemp how a great champion can have many weapons, but maybe none so valuable as a great defense. Never let yourself get out of position when the stakes are high.

The next morning, however, Kemp's strategy was overwhelmed as Schultz used an amazing array of attacks to beat him. Afterward, I took down Iowa's King Mueller, whom Schultz had beaten in his first match. That meant Schultz was undefeated and riding high with his first win over Kemp, the reigning world champ, going into our match. Kemp had already taken out Mueller, which meant if Schultz beat me, I was going home and Schultz was going to the World Cup.

Schultz had the momentum going into our match, but I kept it close. Then he executed a spinning arm throw, where he leached his body around my extended arm and spun his entire weight in a motion that almost took my arm out of its socket. My body went over and exposed my back to the mat. I managed to avoid the fall and got back to neutral position, but Schultz now had a five-point lead, and I had limited use of my right arm. The match ended with Schultz winning 7–3, securing him the spot on the US World Cup team, and me back to deciding what came next.

I knew exactly what I wanted—and what I needed. I chose wrestling at first. It still offered the bigger high for me. As Schultz went on to lose to Vorobiev in the World Cup, I competed at the Canada Cup of International Wrestling and won the bronze medal in my first senior-level international tournament. Schultz then went on to live my dream and win the World Championship later that summer, while my opportunities dried up.

So I chose the other path, and moved up to New York City that summer to start my full-time career as a high-fashion model. I had auditions and shoots by day and wrestling at the exclusive New York

Athletic Club each evening. A fresh start for this Virginia boy in a city where I barely knew anyone.

Maybe the glamour of the bright lights and camera flashes would sate my addiction for the respect of others. As long as I had that, and wrestling, I felt I could control my other addiction to drugs.

BIG CITY DREAMS DELAYED

I ARRIVED IN NEW York City, but I was hardly making it on my own or living the glamorous life. I hadn't booked any gigs while I focused on wrestling again, so I was low on cash, and crashing at my aunt's Upper East Side apartment, which was hardly glamorous and pretty lonely. My aunt was the CFO of the United Nations, and weeks could go by where we didn't see each other. By the time I got home, she was asleep, and when I woke up, she'd be gone again. On the weekends, she usually went to her home in the country. I didn't know many people in the city except for some of my wrestling teammates at my sponsor, the New York Athletic Club on Central Park South, where I was still training for the Olympics. I was meeting some of the most beautiful women in the world, though, and soon working nonstop with professionals in the model business.

I had an open invitation to Studio 54 as a VIP, but I skipped it, which also meant I initially skipped falling into full-blown addiction by steeping myself in the cocaine and other drugs that run that scene. I was using again, but I didn't have much of a network to get ahold of cocaine. Only one girl was a reliable source—someone introduced to me as part of a wealthy family. Her parents had her set up in a Park Avenue apartment, and she always had what I wanted: sex and drugs.

71

Mostly, I drank—for solace and company. I became a regular at an Irish pub, Fitzpatrick's, which was filled with fresh-off-the-boat-looking Irishmen. Sweeney was the manager, and he liked me because he knew some Hanrahans back in Ireland. One evening, a fight broke out and his boys were outnumbered. I jumped at the chance for some action, and quickly took out one guy with a full-on hip toss and then another with a headlock. After that, Sweeney told me to come every night, hang out, drink beer, and if anything got out of hand, he'd pay me to do what I just did. Which was perfect, because while modeling paid well, the summer season jobs were getting farther between, and I couldn't rely on my friend to keep buying the drugs I increasingly felt I needed.

Sure the work I did have was stellar, but it took time to fill my portfolio and get the really big opportunities. Because of the Weber tear sheets, I never did any test shots like most models do, in hopes that they'll eventually get real published editorial pictures shot by the big boys, like Francesco Scavullo and Juan Ramos. I was also working with more of the best photographers in the world like Rico Puhlmann, Mario Testino, Stan Malinowski, Knut Bry, Albert Bray, and Laslo Condor for editorial work published in *Esquire*, *GQ*, and beyond. As a result, Scott had left behind any pretense that I should do low-level work and followed the formula for catapulting his guys to the top. He had one of the faces of the Calvin Klein ads and the latest *GQ* cover superstar. He wanted same for me, so he constantly passed on campaigns that might provide me a chunk of cash but would stifle my ascent as the exclusive new face in the industry.

Scott told me to wait. That's all I was doing, it seemed. Waiting.

Scott did let me go to Warner Brothers when they invited me to their New York office to read for a movie called *Vision Quest*. Someone had submitted my name and said I was a real wrestler. They liked the idea, and they were impressed how easily the lead character, Louden Swain, came off for me. Louden was a wrestler who wanted to be the state champ and get recruited to a top school for a full scholarship. The premise was, he needed to move down a weight class to take on the biggest and best wrestler in the state, Gary Shute. Of course, I told them that this premise made no sense. If Louden was sucking down to a lower weight, he couldn't have a monster like Shute waiting for him. Louden should be the bigger of the two once he made the drop. They ended up passing on me for Matthew Modine, and then passed on me again for the part of Shute. They ended up hiring a big intimidating guy out at the Oregon location.

I waited some more. Soon drinking was not enough. I had found new sources for cocaine, and my habit was growing. I needed money. It was fast becoming my main addiction.

For a while, wrestling remained my anchor to a clean life as I trained for the 1984 Olympic trials. I represented the USA versus the Japanese National Team at the New York Athletic Club's main gymnasium. My nickname at the club was "Hammer," and that day I dropped one by beating Japanese Olympian Naomi Higuchi 8–3 by hitting a five-point high-flying throw to salt away the win and seal our team victory. Rocky Aoki, the Japanese wrestling legend and founder of the Benihana restaurant chain, was watching and congratulated me. So did John Irving, the novelist and former wrestler who used the sport in his books, including *The World According to Garp*. He said he told Bruce Weber that he wouldn't want to photograph a wrestler because we're all ugly.

I told Bruce what John Irving said, and how my agent wanted me to fix my broken nose, because he thought it was now holding me back from work. Bruce Weber disagreed, and to prove it—even though I was still a steep underdog against my countrymen Schultz and Kemp—he first shot *me* for *Interview* magazine's exclusive Olympic hopeful issue. Then he took his outrage out on my agent by taking my perfectly broken nose and booking it and me for *L'Uomo Vogue, British Vogue,* and *Bambini Vogue*—the last one as part of a biker family with kids, shot in the Hamptons.

Bruce's work aside, however, I was getting discouraged. I knew that no cover of a magazine was going to vault me ahead of Schultz and Kemp for an Olympic spot—two guys I respected and who showed me the same, but that I had never come *that* close to beating. Nobody in the world could beat Schultz at this point.

All this was tough for this elite athlete to admit, but it was the truth. I needed one of two things: more gigs to make money to buy drugs and fund my high-fashion lifestyle, or a big break to make my Olympic dream come true.

I got a break, but not in a way I expected. It was one that would actually force me to give up cocaine for months and thus honestly confront what I was doing—what I had become. I should have asked Rocky Aoki for some language lessons, because my agent had set me up for a stint of work in Tokyo. He said he would continue to submit me for work, and when the right campaign came up, I could come back for it. In the meantime, I could do any and all jobs that came my way in the isolated markets of Japan and make big yen without diluting my value in the US.

The Japanese agency wanted me there right away too, so I waited six hours in line at Rockefeller Center to renew my passport, went to the Japanese Embassy to get a work visa, did a few lines, and the next day I was on a flight to Tokyo with my last fifty dollars in my pocket.

◆◆◆

AFTER EIGHTEEN HOURS IN the air, I had just enough cash to pay for a shared bus from Japan's Narita airport to an address where I was supposed to meet an agent from the Askew Model Agency. They would give me some advance money and take me to the apartment I would share with another model. I stopped in the men's room first and found a stall with a hole in the floor. As I squatted low, I wondered if this was a metaphor for where I was or what was to come.

I found my bus and had plenty of time to wonder what I would do if the agent wasn't there to meet me. I had no money, no credit card, the agency was closed, and I didn't know anyone in Japan. Not to mention I didn't speak a word of Japanese.

We finally arrived in Tokyo, and my excitement in seeing the lights and life of the city distracted me. Because when I got off...no one was there to meet me. It was late in the evening, and I used my last coins to call the agency from a payphone. Thankfully, someone was there and told me Jean-Luc was on his way. Ten minutes later, a dark-haired Frenchman in a small red Japanese car jumped out and greeted me excitedly in a thick French accent. As we drove, he told me he was my new manager and handed me an envelope filled with crisp ten-thousand-yen bills, each worth about forty dollars. I started to relax. Tokyo was one of the most expensive cities in the world, and my apartment was in an expensive neighborhood, but I now had a cash advance on my projected earnings under a two-month contract with Askew.

When we arrived at my apartment, I met my flatmate: Marley, a hard-core punk rocker from London with a spiked Mohawk, clunky boots, and a colorful graffiti T-shirt. Shortly after, a half-dozen beautiful female models and a couple of male models joined us, and I got introduced as the new guy from New York. They asked to see my book. *Wow, you worked with Bruce Weber? Where did you do all this Italian Vogue work? Were you in Milan?*

I told them my story and how I never paid my dues in Milan or any European market and worked with all the top photographers in New York from my first shoot onward. *You're going to kill it here in Tokyo.*

What I wasn't going to kill was myself, with cocaine. I learned before I left that drug laws are very strict in Japan and that there is no right to privacy. Apparently that didn't apply to hashish, the aroma and smoke of which filled the air of the apartment as I started to fade from jet lag. I told the crowd I was exhausted and opted to retire to my new bedroom through the sliding door. I looked at the futon on the tatami mat floor and crashed.

◆◆◆

THE FOLLOWING MORNING, JEAN-LUC escorted me and a few other models on a whirlwind of auditions throughout Tokyo. Everywhere people were smoking cigarettes—I saw a man near the Imperial Palace smoking while jogging in a blue and white tracksuit. We went to the top ad agencies in Japan, always taking our shoes off as we entered. As I walked by design tables, I noticed American ads laid out and artists copying them for their own product layout. *They copy everything*, one model said with a nudge as we walked by. They also required the girls to change into bikinis no matter what the job was, just to get off on seeing these beautiful "gaijin" or foreign girls. When my book landed in front of the decision-makers, I watched their eyes and could sense their excitement at my body of work.

We ended up back at the agency that evening, and bookings began to pour in, including a magazine shoot the next morning. I knew some models were still waiting for work and going into deep debt with the agency, between advances and apartment fees. It looked like I'd pay off my two-month advance quickly. I happily joined the other models to hit the nightclubs for dinner, drinks, and dancing. At the first club, Tokio's, we walked to the front of the velvet rope, past the crowd of fashionably dressed Japanese young men and women hoping to get in.

One of the men in line was screaming at the bouncers, and I felt the tension of a fight. A few other men came to the door; their watch hands were all missing fingers. One of the models whispered this was a mark of yakuza, or the Japanese mafia. The gangsters calmed the guy in line and he left. Someone explained this was all a matter of the man "losing face," which I'm told can sometimes lead to life-or-death moments in Japan. As we walked in, I was introduced to the bouncers, gangsters, and club owner. They took my model composite card, nodded approvingly, and let me know I could expect ongoing VIP treatment in their club. Inside Tokio's—and all the best clubs—it was my kind of crowd: beautiful foreign models gathering until the wee hours to have fun, and Japanese girls dancing in groups on the side, watching themselves in the mirror as they moved on the floor.

I am going to kill it here.

◆◆◆

FOR SIX WEEKS, IT was nonstop work and partying in Tokyo, around Japan, and beyond. Every night, the top clubs comped me dinner and more as my stock rose. I appeared in department store and designer ads. I was on billboards. I flew to Guam—landing on the same runway the Enola Gay had departed from to drop the bomb on Hiroshima—to work with acclaimed Japanese photographer Yasushi Handa on a life insurance commercial. Handa is the James Dean of Japan, very cool with a ton of style. Similarly to Bruce Weber, he told me he liked me because I did not look like a typical model and he especially liked my broken nose. I told him I'd actually been stitched up on eight different occasions on my face alone, and he made me tell him the story of each scar, right down to the one on my forehead from diving off my front porch in a homemade Superman cape at age three. We became fast friends, and I became Handa's muse. He had the clout to make the big ad agencies book me for his exclusive campaigns.

I spent Christmas and New Year's in Tokyo that year. At the New Year's Eve party at Tokio's, a guy spiked the sake barrel with acid and caused mass hallucinations. The police were called in. Luckily, it was one of the few nights I didn't drink because I was feeling under the weather. Still, I'm not sure how I would have known—all of Japan seemed like a trip to me.

Yet for its Disney-like feel, Japan also provided one very real moment for me. I had been whisked away a few times to shoot TV commercials on islands around Japan. On one such occasion, I sent my parents a postcard from my luxury hotel on the island of Saipan, where I could see a row of old military tanks rusting in the surf off the beach. I told my parents the beach was the site of the final bloody battle between the US and Japan in World War II. Turned out my dad already knew that.

Dad never talked about his time in the Marines, and I couldn't imagine what it was like for him at seventeen, landing on the beach at Iwo Jima and fighting for his life. I played war in the backyard as a kid, but what did I know about it? Losing battles in football or wrestling rarely meant death. I had learned never to ask about it.

But in his letter back to me, Dad opened up for the first time. He wrote that he had landed on the same island in World War II. He told me how thousands of Japanese women and men jumped off a cliff, committing suicide once the US gained control of the island. They had heard rumors the American GIs would eat them. He told me his division would have invaded Tokyo if the bomb had not stopped the war. In my dad's mind, the bomb that killed so many people in Japan saved his life, because the battle plans for invading mainland Japan included his 4th Marine division and anticipated a million American casualties.

My dad's letter moved me deeply, as I compared it to my polar opposite experience in Japan just forty years later. But his letter helped me understand the few glares I got from people who had lived through the war. My Japanese invasion was nothing but a party. I wondered how that made my dad feel.

It would take more than a few glares to stop me from continuing my Tokyo adventure. But then came a bombshell from my agent in New York. It was the moment he'd been waiting for: Bruce Weber had booked me for the international Gianni Versace campaign.

There was just one problem: Gloria Askew, the British woman who owned the Askew Agency, was not going to give me my ticket to go back. I was only six weeks into my two-month contract, and I had two weeks' bookings and a contract to fulfill. I tried to assure her that this was a win-win. I'd do Versace and return a bigger star, bringing in even more for both of us. But she didn't believe I'd come back and refused to give me my return ticket, locked in the agency safe, or advance me any additional funds for fear I'd run out on her.

The other models tried to console me. This was the fashion industry equivalent of nearing the summit only to be knocked down by a bolder within a few steps of the pinnacle. If I didn't get on a flight to New York by the next night, I would lose the opportunity. Marley had turned out be a gentle natured friend and was especially upset, but he did not have enough money to get me home. No one did. He schemed with the other models on how we could get in the agency safe to get my ticket, but all we ended up doing was what we usually did: clubbing. I had no idea why we picked Raja Court, an upscale club that was kind of stuffy, but at least it had the best food.

We stepped around a Japanese businessman lying in the lobby of the club, vomit all over his face and suit. *This day is just getting better*. I wondered why we hadn't picked something more fun, like Tokio's, but I couldn't stop Marley, who pushed ahead of me as we got inside. I lost sight of him in the sea of suits. He eventually came back beaming. He pulled his hand out of his vintage British military coat pocket and revealed a fist full of yen. *I've got your ticket right here, mate. You're going to go do Versace, baby!*

I didn't know where the money came from and I didn't ask. We contacted a travel agent and paid for my New York ticket in cash, then headed to Tokio's to celebrate.

The key for the next twenty-four hours was to keep my secret until I got out of town. Gloria could have the authorities stop me at Narita Airport for breach of contract, but the models were all on my side and thrilled to see one of their own get one over on Gloria. I got to Narita, and once I cleared security I called Gloria, told her I was gone, and said I was a man of my word. I would come back to finish my contract and make us both more money.

On my flight, I sat next to an elegant woman who owned a boutique in Zurich and had been at the Tokyo fashion shows. We got to talking, and she was fascinated by my escape to shoot Versace. She let me spend much of the flight with my head resting on the soft fur of her coat in her lap. I wanted to look rested and healthy for the biggest shoot of my life. I fell asleep in the perfumed fur of that woman's coat, thinking I would look and feel my best for Versace. I was living more of a fantasy than I thought.

SUMO, THE PUSH TO STAY IN

I LANDED IN NEW York City a day prior to the Versace shoot, hooked up with my Park Avenue girlfriend that evening, and fell right back into full party mode, drinking and doing coke all night long. I did not sleep a wink, and showed up at the studio wired with a cut on the side of my nose.

There were about a dozen male models already there when I arrived—top models and new faces, all of them hoping to emerge as the star of this campaign. We began with an aerobics queen putting our group through a workout as Bruce Weber filmed us. If I thought I looked awful when I showed up, I couldn't imagine how I looked trying to exercise. Bruce and the team *had* to know I was messed up, and I became more and more certain of this as I watched other models get called. I waited and waited near wardrobe as the day dragged on and soon fell asleep on the floor. I woke with someone firmly shaking my shoulder and saying that Bruce was ready for me. No one was left in the waiting room. I was the last shot of the day. *Great.*

The stylist dressed me in a pair of gray and black tweed pants, a bright red Dondi jersey, a Versace leather coat, and the most expensive pair of shoes and gloves I had ever seen. As I walked onto the set, the late evening sun was pouring through the window, mixing with the studio lighting. I felt warm and started to relax. I showed

Bruce the cut on my nose, and he did not seem to care. I didn't care about what most people thought of me in modeling the way I did in wrestling. I wasn't addicted to their approval. I had resigned myself to the fact that I had blown it by staying out all night and that this was probably my last shoot.

Is he just going through the motions? He has the most discriminating eye in the world. He could look right through me.

Bruce had me use the model he had just finished shooting as a prop. I recognized him as the likeable guy appearing in the popular Mountain Dew commercials. *Hey, Johnny, can you put him in a wrestling move?* Sure, I thought to myself—one thing I could always do, wasted or sober, was hit a wrestling move. With both of us shirtless, I leached onto his upper arm and twisted my body into his with a tight fireman's carry lift. Bruce and the crew gasped as I stuck my version of a classic Greco-Roman period human sculpture. Murmurs of *Aww, so beautiful* echoed through the studio. *Ohhh, Johnny, so beautiful, hold that,* Bruce said as his motor-driven camera squealed through his roll of film, an assistant handing him loaded cameras one after another. I was awake and my blood was flowing; I was ready to finish the move with a big throw, but I let the model down gently as we finished the shot.

Bruce then had the studio assistants hand me an Italian cigarette, which I lit and perched between my lips as he shot my profile, kind of James Dean bad-boy style. The smoke made me nauseous.

Is he just messing with me?

We then did a series of shots with me wearing a vibrant red Versace sweater. And just like that we wrapped. *Thanks, Johnny, you were great, beautiful pictures. We'll send the agency over a picture for you to use in your book.* But I knew what would happen next: nothing. It was over. I'd been found out. The Emperor had no clothes except the Versace gloves I wore off the set.

I came to the studio high and left deflated, with just an NYC Transit token in my pocket and the purloined accessories. I decided to stay aboveground and take the bus instead of the subway back to my friend's Upper East Side apartment. I promptly fell asleep, and woke up in an East Harlem neighborhood that I had been told never to wander into, especially at night. I jumped up and pulled the stop cord, and without any other option started walking the seventy blocks back downtown in the dark. I got to a subway and decided to jump the turnstile to get back. It was safer inside, even if the clerk called the cops. He never bothered to look up.

Any lingering hope that I might hear something from my agent regarding the shoot faded over the next few days. I spent those days penniless and wandering near my friend's apartment until I found myself passing Club Magique—a club by night, but earlier in the evening, home to the New York outpost of the famed Chippendale's, where men stripped to down to their G-strings for women in return for tips and drinks.

I had been told by my agent never to work in any club, because if clients saw you working at a regular job, they wouldn't book you for $1,500 a day. Nowhere was that more true than being seen in Chippendale's. But I wasn't sure I *had* a career anymore. And I was broke. And I needed coke. I figured I could make some money in this place for a little while and keep "Magic John" under the radar. It could cost me my livelihood, but it's all about balancing risk and reward, and the highest value reward to me then was cocaine. I needed the score. I went in.

The manager was excited the second he saw me. He had me take my shirt off and dance around to see how I moved. Club dancing had pretty much been my workout for the past six weeks in Tokyo, and I was hired on the spot to join his team of athletes, actors, and desperate models like me.

Chippendale's was a crazy scene. Backstage was like a locker room mashed up with a bar: dudes having a few drinks, busting each other's balls, doing pushups or weights, and getting pumped up to perform, while hundreds of ladies lined up outside the theater, ready for the show. Every night our performance was electrifying and fun for both the ladies and us, and the tips were plentiful. Once the show was over, Club Magique would open as a regular nightclub, and the dancers would put on their jeans and T-shirts and have the rule of the floor. No one in the fashion industry had any idea I worked there, or at least they never told me (because they would have to admit they'd been there too), but I didn't care. I had money for drugs and time to resume training for the Olympics with the New York Athletic Club.

I also made a new friend at Chippendale's, Malone. He shouted, *Hey, you're a barrel-chested Irishman like me, let's hang out.* Every night after the club closed, Malone and I would make the rounds to illegal after-hours clubs with names like "Save the Robots" filled with people who worked the big clubs, giving them and all the lowlifes of the city a place to dance and party from 4:00 a.m. onward. Malone and I watched each other's backs while we were out in many dangerous and precarious situations.

He also became my source for cocaine. Honestly, there was cocaine everywhere—Malone knew where to find it, and people offered it whenever we went out. It had hold of me, and increasingly was the anchor pulling me downward. I was skipping my Olympic training at the New York Athletic Club, and when I did show I was less and less "there." I didn't care if I showed up high.

Neither did Jimmy Mac, a guy from Hell's Kitchen I met at NYAC who took an interest in wrestling and boxing. Jimmy Mac thought it was cool that I was in fashion ads working with beautiful women and also a badass wrestler. One night after a workout, he invited me to go out with him. I pegged Jimmy Mac as some kind of gangster, and when he picked me up in his limo that night, I confirmed it. We rode with his driver downtown and walked up to a nondescript door in a brick building on a darkened side street. The bouncer greeted Jimmy Mac as the owner of the establishment: a bustling illegal gambling den with players from all over town and the world. A world I never knew existed.

Jimmy Mac gave me a couple hundred-dollar bills and told me to go gamble. As I walked around, I saw a few former wrestlers working security. The blackjack dealer was a former national champion wrestler and friend of mine. I sat at his table with a bunch of players who looked like they'd definitely have you killed if you crossed them. I won enough money to piss some of them off. Jimmy Mac gave me a ride home. As we rode, I knew to not ask many questions, but I mentioned the other wrestlers I saw and asked him about working there. I could tell he didn't think it was a great idea. I never asked again. He did, however, invite me to attend the NCAA nationals across the river at the Meadowlands in New Jersey the following week. He would pick me up in his limo again.

I showed up to watch the wrestlers from my former team the only way I knew how those days: high and drunk. It didn't matter that I was supposed to wrestle for the New York Athletic Club and defend our team title at the US Open in a few weeks. I needed a few drinks and bumps of coke before I went to see the matches. I ditched Jimmy Mac and sat far up in the stands in the Penn State section.

As I walked up the aisle, I avoided eye contact and sat in back of everyone. Rows behind. I was there, but not there. I sat down with my giant beer and watched two of my former teammates compete in the national finals, and I cheered like everyone else. But as I cheered, I felt a world away. I was alone, disconnected from my Nittany Lion family and the sport. I knew how far I had fallen. I had entered the tournament the New York Athletic Club put on last December, one that I had easily won before. Sonny Greenhalgh, the club chairman and my biggest benefactor, felt I was still their number-one guy. But in my sorry state, I lost in the finals to a guy from Indiana that I had beaten before. In my own club. In front of all my teammates and our fans. No one was cheering.

No one was cheering for me tonight either. I felt the fans looking over their shoulders as, adding insult to addiction, that night two of my former teammates won national titles and one of them, Carl

DeStefanis, passed me to become the winningest wrestler in Penn State history. *They know who I am. They know I am high. Isn't that Hanrahan? The former winningest guy in Penn State history? The first guy to get one hundred wins? The wrestler who became a model... jacked out of his mind? What happened to him?*

No, they didn't think that.

No one does anymore. No one here gives a crap about who I am – about who I was. Unlike my last night at Penn State, I'm not a wrestler tainting his legacy like a junkie. I'm just a junkie tainting a wrestling event. I'm history. Old news. The one who never made it to the top of the Rec Hall wall as a national champion. The one who couldn't beat Dave Schultz or Lee Kemp at the Olympic Trials. The one who betrayed the sport he loved. The one who let his new addiction destroy the old one.

I had come within a point of defeating the mighty Soviet World medalist. But I now knew I was an addict and completely out of reach of a lifetime dream—I knew it, and I abandoned the Olympic Trials. My coach, Sonny, searched frantically for me at LaGuardia airport, but I was nowhere to be found. I hadn't exactly fallen off the face of the Earth—my face was in a number of current ads and even featured in the current *Interview Magazine*'s Olympic issue. I didn't show up for the trip to the US Open to defend my club's title, and we lost the title to the Iowa Hawkeye Club.

Sonny did not hide his disappointment. When he saw me the following week at the club, he lit into me. *Hanrahan, where the hell were you? I had your freaking plane ticket ready. You let us down, man. We lost a team title because of you. Your points could have made the difference.* But there wouldn't have been any points from me. I wouldn't have made it out of the first round. I just shook my head and left.

I can't come back anymore. I can't compete anymore.

My Olympic trials were finished. There was no way I could take on Schultz and Kemp. And for the first time I felt something: regret for how I had let myself go. I decided to let go. No more thinking that I could give up the life I led, train my ass off, and learn new techniques to defend against Schultz's barrage of attacks. I thought about my days in the workout room at Penn State. There were windows that looked out to the students in the hallway. We'd work so hard, there'd be puddles of sweat in there, and a fog of condensation from all the body heat. I'd look up and I'd see the faces behind the steamed-up windows watching us work. We had their respect. *I had their respect.* Now I was the one on the outside, in a fog, looking in.

I decided to resign. I was paying the price for cocaine, not the price for competing. Kemp and Schultz deserved the Olympics. I did not. I could not be Rick Sanders and party all the time, get the girls, and still win an Olympic medal. I used to be the first in the room and the last to leave and still party my ass off. It was all about feeding my ego. I loved those days. Loved those cheers. I fed off the crowd. I fed off the glory. I fed off the women that threw themselves at me. Women don't throw themselves at losers, and I couldn't take another disappointing loss.

It didn't matter that my photo in *Interview Magazine* proclaimed me an Olympic hopeful. I had no hope. I hadn't been sacrificing what I knew I had to sacrifice, but I hadn't been willing to quit until now. Now I had lost all the control wrestling gave me. I had lost the winning mindset. No one had actually beaten me but me. It was all a story I told myself. How do I know I wouldn't have beaten Schultz? I didn't. I just convinced myself. Took the easy way out and let the drugs comfort me. My excuse to run away.

Dear Wrestling,

Please excuse John Hanrahan for throwing in the towel. He's too busy being a model/ full-fledged addict to care about his addiction to you anymore.

Sincerely,
Cocaine

In the days following my decision, I felt hollow. There was an empty space inside me for the first time since I was seven. I wondered how other athletes who had retired because they had to, not because they wanted to, filled the void. If I had ever had a long-term relationship, I might know if this is what it feels like when the love of your life leaves. But she hadn't left. I had sabotaged this relationship. Pushed her out the door. *Sorry, Wrestling, I've got a new girl now. Her name is Cocaine, and she makes me feel good. We're gonna party it up while I do more endorsements and magazine covers and surround myself with the most beautiful women in the world. She gives me everything I can't have with you.*

But the real truth. The real truth was, I gave up. I couldn't win, so I ran away into something else.

But where could I go? My wrestling career was over. My shots would never get published for the Versace campaign. I knew how many top models were there that day and the shape I'd showed up in. They deserved it. I didn't. Unlike Sinatra, I wasn't going to make it in New York. There was one place I knew I could escape, and even escape the drugs that were filling my body for a while, make some good money, and it wasn't Chippendale's.

I would go back to Tokyo.

♦♦♦

AFTER THE VERSACE SHOOT, Bruce had kept his promise. His office sent my agent some of my pictures to use in my book before the campaign was published. My agent made a new composite card with the pictures, and I had him send the shots over to Japan. I then called Gloria Askew in Tokyo and asked her if she had seen the Versace shots. I told her I was calling to keep my word. I had offers to work with top agencies in Milan and Paris, but it was important to me that I come back and make good on the last two weeks of my contract.

Gloria had seen the shots, and she was ecstatic. She told me my value had skyrocketed with those pictures and had a pending international campaign in play. She was more than happy to put the past in the past, booked my round-trip ticket to Tokyo, and had a new promotional card of me printed while I was on the plane.

I was going back to my Disneyland—my "Magic Kingdom" where I felt I ruled the world and could run away from what haunted me in New York. Tokyo was the fantasy that made me believe everything was going to be okay.

And that's exactly how it played out. From the moment I arrived, I was a star again. A new agency rep was on time to pick me up and delivered me to an even nicer apartment, which I shared with an Italian superstar who had worked the great markets of the world, was the epitome of cool, and had a legendary reputation as a lady's man. The work rolled in. Yasushi Handa, still Japan's best photographer and the only one whose work could actually further my reputation worldwide, booked me for anything he could. The nightlife was even better than before, as celebrities and rock groups that came through Tokyo hung out with us.

I could be anything I wanted to be in Japan. I was an equestrian riding a horse in a Polo campaign (even though I had never ridden one in my life). I was a surfer on the beach (which I had never even tried, but I jumped in the freezing cold Pacific and worked with the board so it looked like I was riding the waves). One night I got invited to a sumo stable's banquet by a US wrestler who was working in Tokyo. Turns out, I was more than a guest: I was a guest of honor. That meant they put me in the wide canvas belt that wraps around your crotch and waist, the uniform of sumo.

I soon realized that they wanted me to battle a sumotori from their stable in front of the hundreds of people at the banquet. I had enough sake in me not only to try, but also to play it up and have some fun with it. They introduced me, and as I got to the low, long table that led to the stage, I flipped onto my hands and walked on my hands to the front of the room on top of the table, past the people sitting on the floor. As I got to the last table, I hit a handspring to my feet, to raucous approval and applause from the mostly Japanese crowd.

My opponent, an up-and-coming rikishi who outweighed me by eighty pounds, came to the front of the room dressed in his garb and ready to go head-to-head. I was unsure whether this was just an exhibition or a real competition, but this kid was huge, so I needed to be prepared. The judge waved his arm and began the initial lock-up. I felt comfortable to hold that position until I knew what was going on, and when I felt his aggression, I baited him and wrapped an inside trip, dropping him to his butt and thus winning the match. He left the room, and I took the traditional victor's crouch position and was handed cash. The crowd cheered. I got the place of honor next to the sumo stable's legendary *yokozuna*, or grand champion. The huge man nodded approvingly. He told me through a translator that I would always have an invitation to be part of this stable. He then presented me with a sumo belt to keep.

I have it made here—and now I have a championship belt to prove it. I asked them to hold the belt there, to keep it safe for me when I came back.

As I got home that night, I realized that was the closest I was going to get to any championship. My world championship and Olympic dreams were dead, and I was grateful and angry that there was no cocaine to be found. This was my life now. The closest I was going to get to the Olympics was a staged battle between models as athletes for a Japanese *TV Guide* cover. Reaffirming the fantasy and how far removed I was from wrestling, I was dressed as a runner. I'm not even fast.

Months later, while working on a remote island starring in a commercial for a Japanese sports beverage and listening to Armed Forces radio updates of the 1984 Olympic Games in Los Angeles, I heard that Dave Schultz had won the Olympic gold medal in my weight class. I told myself I was genuinely happy for Dave and consoled my lingering nostalgia and disappointment with my

Japanese fame. Dave might get the Wheaties box, but he wasn't going to be getting endorsements like I was.

It sounded like an excuse even to me. *I'm seeing the world. I'm working in places that Dave can't even imagine. At least I'm here. I'm doing this TV commercial, and he's probably not even going to get to do a TV commercial, because nobody cares about Olympic wrestling.* One big, rambling rationalization. I felt pathetic, but without any cocaine available, it was all I had to take away the pain in Japan. And I was all about taking away the pain—or running away from it to find the adrenaline, the rush I needed. That had been modeling in Japan, but the façade was wearing thin. Modeling wasn't real. I was never myself in front of the camera, and no amount of partying made me feel any better. There was no danger like there was with wrestling. There was no comparison. What's the worst that can happen? I take a bad picture?

Dave's victory was the first chink in my Disneyland armor, but it was soon followed by an even bigger dent.

My friend Stefan from Sweden was one of my biggest nightlife partners in crime. We could do no wrong. When we ran up on the karaoke stage and started singing Frank Sinatra, badly, the audience didn't dare do anything but applaud. But Stefan had a bad habit of taking a cab home and skipping out on the fare. One night, he got dropped near our neighborhood at the main intersection, next to an all-night pharmacy. He bolted from the car and ran around a building and up the outer stairs ten floors to the roof. These other cabbies, yakuza types that hung out at that corner by the pharmacy, saw what happened and tracked Stefan down on top of the building.

The story I heard was that as the cabbies climbed the stairs to the roof, Stefan tried to hide by climbing up the water tower ladder, but he was spotted and had to jump off the tower, back onto the roof. The cabbies had him. They grabbed him and dragged him to the roof's edge and threw him off—ten stories down to the alley, where he died. The story the cabbies told the police was that he jumped, and it went in the books as a suicide, which was ridiculous. No one was more full of life than Stefan. I laid in the chalk outline of his body the next morning in grief. He left a pregnant girlfriend behind.

Stefan's death shook me. While I was still unable to find cocaine, I started drinking more than I ever had and smoking a lot of hashish. After a night of excessive drinking, I took a pill another model gave me. I had no idea what it was, but I woke up bloody in my apartment with a note in broken English, a yogurt drink, and a vending muffin beside me. I had no memory of the night, but from the note and talking to my friends later, I learned I had blacked out, crashed my body through a storefront window, and cut my shoulder. My friends were able to put me in a cab and get me back to my apartment. They said I was screaming I wanted Kentucky Fried Chicken, and that's why they got me something from the vending machines on the corner.

Around the same time, I was out with Handa, who often drove me in his red Ferrari to authentic establishments I would have never have found otherwise. One night in a small restaurant bar, an old man was glaring at me. I asked Handa what was up, and Handa asked the man and translated for me. The man said how much hatred he had for me, and all Americans, from his family's experience in the war. At first, I took some offense, since they started the fight, but I remembered what my father told me and stayed silent.

After we left, I found myself still thinking about the man— and I had more than just a new awareness of the deep unresolved issues between our countries. There were unresolved issues in me, too. I had spent four very productive months earning big yen in my fantasy world, but how long could I go on like this?

A few days later, the new Versace campaign hit, and to my astonishment, I was *the shot* that defined the campaign. Everyone else was left on the cutting room floor. The powers that be at the brand had picked me as the face of Versace for the season, and I was suddenly featured in every fashion magazine around the world, as well as billboards and boutique posters.

I had to get back to New York City.

I'M THAT GUY

I ARRIVE IN NEW York City, and all I see is myself. My Versace picture is everywhere.

The shot they used looked much better than the outtake photo I had been given. I was usually my own worst critic, whether it was a wrestling match or modeling pictures. Doing that made me better at what I did. I self-edited my portfolio to make sure I maintained a level of allure and mystique without compromising the qualities that made me appealing to advertising clients, not just another pretty face. When a client looked at my book, I would watch his or her eyes as they moved through to try and gauge what they were looking at. But even my most brutal inner critic was happy with this shot.

My image was on subways, on billboards, at all the boutiques that sold Versace, and in *Vogue* and all the magazines. People pointed at me on the bus when they saw my face in the ad next to me. I was a top model, and it felt great. And I knew only one way to make it feel even better.

Within weeks, I was walking right past the bouncers and into Studio 54 carrying a cookie jar full of cocaine.

THE PLEASURE DOME

WHILE I WAS IN Japan, Malone gained a connection with a Colombian man who had a drugstore in East Harlem. Well, it was a bodega in front, but in back it was a drugstore with only one drug for sale, and it wasn't aspirin. Malone and I would ride uptown in a cab, passing my face all over the bus stop light boxes along the street, until all the signs and ads disappeared across 125th Street. I hadn't been to Harlem since I fell asleep on the bus after the Versace shoot, but this time it was for a good cause. I was ready to party.

Malone told the cab to drop us off on a corner a block away, and we started walking. I immediately felt self-conscious. I wasn't dressed right for these streets. I looked fashionable. I felt like an easy target. I resolved to wear my old Army jacket the next time I came.

We entered the bodega and walked past the girl at the register. The shelves were basically empty except for a few bags of chips and Brillo pads. *People must know what's going on here, right?* But I didn't care. I kept my eyes forward. We got to the back of the store and stood in front of a glass mirror with a door next to it. When the door opened, I met Poppi for the first time.

Poppi was not a dude you wanted to mess with, especially as two guys you also did not want to mess with flanked him. In front of

Poppi and his henchmen, sitting there in all its glory, was a block of cocaine getting cut up for sale.

I think Poppi got a kick out of us: two white-guy addicts willing to face their fears and come all the way to Harlem to buy his shit. He sold me my first bag, and we thanked him and grabbed a gypsy cab back downtown. No regular cab would ever be up in this part of Harlem. No one from downtown would ever be in this part of Harlem unless they had a good reason. Malone and I started getting high in the backseat. Then we ran around town wide awake for three days, celebrating my Versace success.

A few weeks later, I was making good money from my increased bookings as the new Versace star. I took much of what I earned, put on my Army jacket, and started heading up to Poppi on my own to fill the cookie jar I carried into Studio 54 and fuel the fun at my apartment, which became known as the Pleasure Dome. The Pleasure Dome was on West Fifty-Seventh Street between Ninth and Tenth avenues, and I shared the place with Susie, the twin sister of an old Penn State girlfriend, who'd needed a roommate. She was down in Philadelphia a lot and needed someone to offset the cost of maintaining a Manhattan pad. The location was perfect and the relationship chaste—Susie was like a sister to me—so I jumped at the chance.

Studio 54 was blocks away from the Pleasure Dome and became one of my regular hangouts. It was an exclusive perk to be able to have the bouncer part the sea of wannabes waiting outside and lift the red velvet rope to usher me in free of charge. They never looked inside the jar.

This was the glamorous life I lived now: a model VIP comped into Studio 54 or Area, Tunnel, Heartbreaks, Palladium, China Club. The spotlights on the dance floor were a long way from those I aspired to wrestle under at Falls Church High School, but at least I had a crowd that wanted me again. There were no wrestlers in my way to win this competition, just a sea of beautiful people:

fashionistas, artists, celebrities, drag queens, and the lucky few who got to pay the hefty admission to our party. Nothing was off-limits inside. The bathrooms were orgies of drugs and sex. The whole vibe made me feel like the coolest guy in the world. If I was going to be high, this was the time and place to be. When the clubs closed, we headed back to the Pleasure Dome for the after-hours party. It was a rotating cast of characters, including my friend Malone. We got the name from the movie *Mad Max: Beyond Thunderdome*, only in our case, two men enter and then…more men enter and women enter and we all drink and get high until the sun comes up.

As daylight filled New York, I'd sit on the windowsill and look for the VJs entering the MTV studio across the street. On weekends, we'd stay up straight into the next day, quieting only for a little bit when the neighbors banged on the walls, ceiling, or floor. They were just jealous, and nothing stopped the party for long—not even work. One guy I knew who worked in fashion got so high doing cocaine he couldn't function for a huge job the next day. Unlike me, who now knew I could fake it in front of the camera and still win Versace, this guy worked off camera as a top makeup artist and could never do his work this high without repercussions. If he showed up high, he would get fired. He looked at me. *I know what I gotta do. I'm going to get out of this.* He told me later he went back to his apartment, got on his bike like he always did to get to the job, but this time barreled into a bunch of garbage cans kamikaze style, cutting himself open in the process. He then went to the emergency room and got stitched up so he could have a good excuse for calling in and missing work.

He didn't stop using. No one did. If I ever felt life was out of control or that what he had done was a sign things had gone too far, I ignored it and took my modeling money to Poppi. Life was a party, and I was hosting it. This was the fuel for my ego, replacing the adoration of my fans and wins on the mat. The glamour of my nights was matched by my rise in demand as a model. I had ditched my agent with thanks for all he did and switched over to the illustrious

Ford Modeling Agency, the best in the business, with swank offices on Fifty-Seventh Street.

They leveraged my Versace appearance all they could. I got the cover of a new men's magazine, *MGF*, and I showed up to shoot with photographer Christopher Makos wasted. They told me to look young and smile. Be innocent. So I did. They couldn't see the addiction in my eyes. They just saw my boyish face, the only remnant of this All-American boy. Same thing happened at shoots with photographers like Mario Testino and brands like Perry Ellis, Swatch, DiMitri, Wilson, Henry Grethel, Suzuki. In between, Ford sent me out for catalog work with J. C. Penney, Macy's, Saks Fifth Avenue, Bloomingdale's, and Sears to fill their thousands of catalog pages. I did the cover of a romance novel that was booked by coincidence with my old high school girlfriend, who had become the queen of this genre. She usually worked with Fabio. None of the catalog or Fabio-like work was going to further my career, but it paid $150 hour and $1,200 per day, and I put every dollar I could spare into the Poppi Cocaine Scholarship Fund for Wasted Models in Harlem.

With bags of coke handy, life became an even more debauched series of events capped by late nights in the Pleasure Dome. I hung with *Playboy* centerfolds. I had dinner with Andy Warhol, soft-spoken and seemingly shy, and Grace Jones, elegant in the sheer hooded top that framed her chiseled face. I yachted to the Bahamas to spend time at a countryside castle with a beautiful Italian divorcée. Took private planes to Key West getaways. I got flown out to LA and sent on a cruise ship for a one week shoot for an Italian designer, and we partied at every port all the way to Acapulco. When one of the female models climbed into my bunk the first evening, it became the Love Boat. I had no interest in love. I had only one love now—the one that made me feel great and made others want to be around me. Sure, it was harder to get cocaine in Mexico, but I managed to score some on the beach and use it in the ocean waves, in case the

Federales on the beach closed in. It was shit coke, but I needed it and ignored the risk of doing it in plain sight of those cops.

I had long ago stopped caring about repercussions and took bigger and bigger risks. On a weeklong trip to the Florida Keys for a print and film campaign—the solo male model working with top female swimwear models—the director wanted me to lean on one of the hanging ropes. *How about I climb up?* I said. *You can do that?!* He was shocked. *Yeah! I can climb up it upside down, too!* I proceeded to do so as he clicked the shutter. Suddenly, the rope broke from its grappling hook and my head came crashing down to the pier, knocking me unconscious. When I came to, a large crowd had gathered, and I was helped to my feet. Two EMS guys were asking me questions: *What day is it? Do you know where you are? Are you seeing double?* I thought it was a trick question because the EMS guys were identical twins. I was rushed to the hospital in Marathon Key and put under observation, but was soon released with a concussion diagnosis and instructions to take it easy.

Instead, I had a Florida "friend" drive down from Miami to deliver me coke.

The only time I had any perspective about how far gone I was and how far I had fallen was when I got a call from Coach Lorenzo at Penn State, informing me that I had been chosen to be inducted into the Eastern Wrestling Hall of Fame. The ceremony would be at the league championship. *Will you come down?* I thought about it. I still held wrestling in high regard—one of purity, character, and the ancient Greeks' ideal of an athlete. I even looked forward to it for a moment. But instead I asked Coach to accept the award on my behalf. I had left that world behind. The cheers of that crowd held no sway over the current me.

The next week, in the mail, I received a beautiful plaque with my photo and my accomplishments engraved on it. I fell into a deep depression. I remembered what I'd felt around those fans at the NCAAs in the Meadowlands last year. I remembered walking away from the New York Athletic Club—walking away from my dreams on the mat. Running away. Only this time, I couldn't fill the hollow feeling with days of modeling and nights of partying. As if I needed another sign of how far I had fallen from wrestling grace, an unwelcome ghost from that past also reached out to me: gladiatorum, the dreaded strain of the herpes virus that lived within me since a match in Pittsburgh, had flared up on my face. I told the agency that I was "booked out," or unavailable, for jobs or castings. I unplugged the phone and stayed inside getting high for three days while my face healed. Every time I thought about what the heck I was doing or caught a glimpse of my face, I got higher.

By Friday afternoon, the virus had run its course and the ugly lesions would be gone soon. I plugged in the phone. It startled me when it rang immediately. It was Ford. *Thank God you answered. Bruce Weber is shooting in Vegas and wants you out there.* A limo arrived to take me to the airport, and I was off to Caesar's Palace in Vegas for a three-day *Vogue* shoot.

Bruce took us to dinner with the Elvis and Marilyn Monroe impersonators, who were dating each other. He entertained us and made sure we all got to know each other before we climbed into a motor home the next day to change into who he wanted us to be. Men dressed like fight gangsters and women dressed Vegas sexy, we hit the Vegas Strip and the high roller suites. We sat front row in shows like Siegfried & Roy and with the showgirls backstage. I looked at the women around me and thought about who I wanted to celebrate with back in the room.

That's when I saw Kirsten for the first time. She was beautiful, blonde, and exactly what I looked for in a woman. Then I heard she was with another model. I was interested in conquest, not competition, so I picked another model from the group.

Yet something about Kirsten made me feel different. I thought something might happen if I stuck around. But Bruce and his crew were headed to Santa Monica. I went with them to spend a few days in LA before flying back to New York. I never got her number.

Once I got back, I fell deeper into cocaine than I ever had before and blew through any money I had. I couldn't be without the coke, even when my heart was racing so quickly that I felt I needed to go to the ER. I made my way to St. Luke's Roosevelt Hospital, but before I went inside, I placed a bag of coke in the crack of a phone booth next to the entrance, hoping it would be there when I came out. I went in and told the receptionist that I was on drugs and my heart was racing. They had me lie on a gurney. The PA blared: *Open heart surgery team, please report to ER, code red!* My heart raced even faster; I was petrified the code red was for me.

Minutes went by, and I relaxed until a doctor wheeled me into an exam room, took my vitals, and had me lie there for hours. *Mr. Hanrahan, my diagnosis is you are fine. You're a drug user and you had an anxiety attack. Stop using drugs.*

For a New York minute, I listened. Before I went back to the Pleasure Dome, I left the hospital, walked right past the phone booth with my hidden bag of coke, and into St. Paul's. I knew the story of Paul as one of the greatest converts to Christianity: how he was struck down by a bolt of light and blinded for three days before becoming a great messenger of light and hope. I kneeled and prayed for forgiveness and strength. The next day, I called my sister Teri, the nurse, about getting help. Teri knew I was in bad shape—had known for a while—and she let me know Dad knew too. With his health insurance policy, I could be covered for thirty days in rehab.

I was not St. Paul, ready to receive the message. Instead of seeing this as an answered prayer, my first reaction was anger. *Dad knew. Dad! I didn't need him to know! Did she sell me out?* Teri had been the first in my family to know I had a cocaine problem. The first year I moved to New York City, I came home for Thanksgiving. I was doing coke throughout that holiday weekend and wasn't eating anything. Teri had seen enough addicts at her job to understand what was happening.

She later showed me a page from her diary that confirmed she knew long before the holiday. She just didn't know what to do.

Did that mean she ratted me out to Dad? Then again, my younger brother Patrick had seen what life was like for me when he visited me in New York. No, it wasn't Patrick. He got a kick out of going to the nightclubs, and he trusted everything would be okay.

Teri was never one to back down. She was tougher than I ever was. When she was fourteen, she disappeared one Sunday afternoon walking home from church. Local detectives and police officers filled our house. *Where the hell was she?* She turned up that evening bursting through our front door crying. A man had jumped out from behind a tree, put a knife to her throat, and abducted her. She escaped from his clutches as he pulled up to a convenience store and ran home, hiding from the road the whole way. I listened from my room as she painfully recounted her story to the detectives before being taken to the hospital.

I lost part of my trust in humanity that day, but Teri didn't. She was the most human person I knew, and if she was worried and Dad was worried, then the least I could do was not yell at her. My anger subsided.

So I pretty much lied. I told her I felt comforted by her words and would think about it. Maybe I thought about it until I was sober. Then my pride convinced me that accepting anyone's help would be admitting I was unable to care for myself. I had an image to maintain. Any memory of church teaching that pride cometh before the fall was clearly gone. But who am I kidding—pride always got in the way of my fall.

Five days later, I went back to that phone booth by St. Luke's Roosevelt Hospital. My little bag was still there. I grabbed it and fell full-blown into using again.

NOTED

THE NIGHT AFTER I went back to St. Luke's Roosevelt, something must have felt different inside me. I started carrying around notes in my pocket for when my body was found.

A few hours into my high, I'd find a piece of paper, tear off the corner, and write something. The cops would find the note in the watch pocket of my jeans when they found the rest of my personal effects: an empty plastic bag of cocaine and cut straws.

Messages to my family: *If I die don't blame yourself for somehow failing to save me—you didn't do anything wrong.*

A message for Teri: *If I die don't blame yourself for somehow failing to save me.*

Messages to my parents, because of their Catholic faith and feelings about suicide: *I didn't commit suicide. The drugs killed me.*

I *was* praying to God, but I didn't write a note to God. I wasn't writing to get into Heaven.

When I didn't die at the end of my latest binge, I would empty my pocket of bags and straws, and I'd find the notes and read them. Disgusted with myself, I'd gather up the notes and all the drug paraphernalia, clean off the tabletop, and throw the pile down the incinerator chute in the hallway.

Then it would start over again. The urge. New bags, new straws, new notes.

I had been afraid before of dying while binging on drugs, pushing myself to the limits. But my night at St. Luke's Roosevelt, feeling like my heart was going to explode and then returning to chase that high even after Teri reached out, made me believe death was closer than ever before.

Meanwhile, a part of my modeling career was dying too. Opportunities for male models gracing the covers dried up when Washington Redskins' quarterback Joe Theismann appeared on the cover of *GQ*. From that moment, the magazine, and then more magazines after that, stopped using models on covers. It was only celebrities. I had shot a potential *GQ* cover with Rico Puhlmann that was shelved for good.

Later that same week, while I was at a tequila bar on the Upper West Side, my car was broken into and the bag with my portfolio in it was stolen. I searched the neighborhood and confronted thugs hanging out in a darkened park, to no avail, and I went home that night figuring my modeling career was over. I only had some mini books left, with copies of a few of the valuable original tear sheets in my stolen book. The next afternoon, a teacher in Harlem called Ford. One of the girls in her class had my book and told her she got it from her older brother's friends. The teacher had looked at it and saw the "If found…reward" sticker.

They got their reward, and I got another sign to clean up. I prayed for the strength to listen this time. The next day, as thick fog blanketed the streets and rain began to fall on New York City, I returned to St. Paul's Church near St. Luke's Roosevelt Hospital. I had felt a hope of healing my first night there, when Teri called with an offer of help that I couldn't bring myself to take. I prayed for strength to fight this disease. I sought healing radiation through the light of the holy candles burning in the chapel. The midday mass was in session, and I shook off some of my dampness and took a seat in a pew beside a homeless man. I slumped a bit as John Collins—or Father Jack, as he was known—came to the altar and began to give his sermon. His loud, charismatic voice made me sit up and take notice. I had never felt the energy or presence of a priest like this. It was as if he had just walked off a stage ten blocks south on Broadway and jumped on the stage here to give another overwhelming performance. His words spoke directly to me, as if he had been following me through the mean streets of my addiction and adventures in debauchery. He understood my pains. I felt the light. I felt his healing as if God wrapped Himself around me. I felt hope—a seed of light planted inside me.

I met Father Jack after the mass on the front steps, and he said he would pray for me. But as I wandered off, I felt the light slipping away. I knew—*knew*—I needed to fight to keep hope alive. The portfolio and Father Jack had been signs. I had lost control of my addiction and increasingly my career in New York City. I was alone again. But instead of seeking help, I locked the door on the Pleasure Dome and did what I had done before.

Like the Bruce Springsteen song "Born to Run," I ran away.

RUNNING FROM REALITY

A TOP AGENCY IN Paris called Best One wanted me to work their market, and I jumped at the opportunity to leave New York for a while. Ford coordinated everything, and I hopped on a flight to Orly International, stopped at the agency to meet the bookers, got set up in a nice big apartment with a view of Notre-Dame Cathedral, and started working immediately. The ultimate highlight was a New Year's Eve fashion show I was featured in at the Eiffel Tower, which was broadcast live across France. My nights in Paris were spent dancing and drugging at the ultra-fashionista nightclub Les Bains Douches.

Like so many Americans before me, I found the architecture of Paris amazing and the people basically rude with little patience if you could not speak their language. Then I met a beautiful French woman on the street who rekindled my faith in her people. She taught me the history and significance of the public fountains throughout the city and the work of Jean Beausire. When Paris had trouble supplying enough water to its growing population in the late seventeenth century, Beausire created the city's first drinking fountains: usually small and set against a wall, with a niche and a single spout pouring water into a small basin—a dignified and elegant solution. We had no more than a long walk, a passionate afternoon in her bedroom, and a delicious dinner together before I had to move on from Paris that night, but my decision to run was now paying extra dividends. For the first time in a long time, I felt a connection to a woman, not simply a conquest.

After Paris came Milan. I was set up with the top agency, Fashion, and put up in a small hotel with an American roommate who promptly introduced me around and took me to the models' club of choice. I immediately spotted Kirsten, the model I'd worked with in Vegas. She screamed when she saw me and gave me a big hug, and before I could say *Can I buy you a...*she introduced me to her boyfriend. Still, we had a connection, and she spent the rest of my stay in Europe calling me for advice about leaving him. I enjoyed talking to her even though I wouldn't tell her what to do. I knew she should leave him. This guy in Milan was worse than the airhead surfer dude I met in Vegas: arrogant and a fellow addict. But I did not want to push her. If I was going to be with her, I couldn't ever have her say, *I left that guy because you told me to, and it was all for this? I never should have listened to you.*

Not wanting to lose the light that Father Jack rekindled in me, I found a church in my Italian neighborhood and sat shoulder to shoulder in the crowded pews and listened. I didn't understand a word of Italian or Latin, but the words comforted me. I still had that quiet voice inside of me—faint, but not yet drowned out. I gave thanks to God for allowing me to survive this far given what I had done.

I had run away from my problems, but maybe, just maybe, I had a chance to fight for redemption.

The next day, I discovered I had been set up on an exclusive long-term job with Versace.

EUROPEAN ESCAPE

THE DIRECTOR OF OPERATIONS picked me up in Milan. We drove north out of the city, through some of the most beautiful countryside I had ever seen, to Gianni Versace's manufacturing headquarters. Gianni gave me a personal tour of the operation and introduced me to everyone at the facility, from the ladies who sew the garments to the bistro attendants. Finally, he told me about the job: working eight-hour days, five days a week, at their headquarters. I'd be working alongside six of the top female models at exclusive shows for international buyers. In other words, a dream job. Was this really happening?

Donatella Versace's husband Paul and I hit the road back to Milan and stopped along the way for a few beers. The next week, I began working daily as the only male model sharing a large open changing room with a half-dozen beautiful female models from around the world. I became their big brother and personal confidant, helping them snap a bra on or whatever they needed to show off the designs in our mini fashion shows. I knew this was all a fantasy, but it was my fantasy, and I was lucky to have it. Every day on my way to work, I would pass guys who came to Milan hoping to become models and were now stranded and living homeless in the park, still desperately hoping for a break or to get just one booking—one sliver of the recognition I had. The majority of models in this town were fortunate if they booked a one-hour job in a week, but they still held onto the dream that they'd get that *one job* that gave them what I had on my first day in this business: a tear sheet that would catapult them to the big time.

I was who they wanted to be. I remember having a thought similar to the one I'd had in Japan, when I heard the Olympic results: Dave Schultz didn't have this. No wrestler ever did. If the boys from Penn State could see me now... In wrestling, your rewards were a direct reflection of the work you put in meshed with God-given ability. In this business, you may have been blessed with God-given looks, but you had little control over your success. I had it, and for the first time in a year, I felt relaxed and in control. I made sure I enjoyed the rewards, exploring Italy's treasures. On one trip, Kirsten, my roommate, and I went down to Venice. I was particularly moved by the massive and hauntingly beautiful painting of *The Last Supper* by Jacopo Tintoretto in the Basilica di San Giorgio Maggiore. I knew the painting from my art history classes.

Maybe seeing the painting was prophetic, because my Milan job was ending too. Any day would be my last meal in Italy. Unsure of what to do next, Kirsten talked me and my roommate into going to Switzerland to work the Zürich market. She had modeled there before and was going back with her boyfriend. My roommate and I got set up with an agency in Zürich, called Time, recommended by our agent in Milan, and we spoke to the manager by phone. *Come right up! No no, no need to get a special work visa or anything. Just come!*

We arrived at the Zürich train station the next day and met a local guy, our age, who invited us to stay at his apartment. We instantly began doing castings all over Zürich. I even remembered to say hi to the woman whose perfumed coat had nuzzled me on my first flight home from Tokyo. In the evenings, we'd get together with Kirsten and her boyfriend and go to a bar or maybe a movie. We wore out our welcome with the local guy and checked into a hotel as the bookings rolled in. I soon had work set for a week straight, starting with two jobs in one day. The first was a department store advertisement, and I got my voucher for the work signed by the client. Vouchers were a common practice on any job in any market. It was simply a billing record you returned after the work was done to get paid through your agency. I thanked them and hustled via taxi to a studio on the outskirts of Zürich for my second job: the cover for an upcoming Swiss *TV Guide* magazine, with me recreating Rodin's famous sculpture *The Thinker*. I nailed the pose, told everyone I was looking forward to seeing it on the newsstands the following week, got my voucher signed, grabbed my black shoulder bag with my portfolio and voucher books, and walked to the nearby train station. I was ready to celebrate. First, I'd head back to the agency, turn in my vouchers, and get paid.

I never saw the magazine. As I sat on a bench at the train stop, two men approached me and wanted to see my ID. They identified themselves as agents of the law, the Swiss Starsky and Hutch. I showed them my passport. They then searched my bag and started looking through my portfolio book. I wasn't hiding any drugs and had done nothing illegal, or so I thought, so I didn't even flinch. That's when they spotted my job vouchers and demanded to see my work visa. I told them to check with my agent, and I was immediately arrested. I asked them what my rights were. *Rights? You have no rights.*

Starsky threw me in the vehicle, and I was transported to the station. As I waited, I heard Hutch connect with my booker from the agency. I figured this would all be cleared up and they'd share a laugh with me about the misunderstanding. When they hung up, they weren't laughing. The agency, covering its ass, denied representing me. *But the vouchers I have, with their company name on it?* No response.

I was driven to the Zürich jail and put in lockup. I wasn't scared, only confused. *Who gets arrested in Switzerland? Isn't this a neutral country?* I was put in a concrete cell and given a pack of cigarettes, dark bread, and meat spread. The thick walls of the cellblock echoed with screams and arguments in German as I fell asleep. Days passed before I went in front of a judge.

Why did you come to our country?

I had been rehearsing my answer—a truthful answer, since it was the truth that got me off in my last appearance with a judge. *Before I left the United States for Europe, my mother, whose family is Swiss German, told me to make sure to get to Switzerland if I have the opportunity, because that's where our ancestors are from. So while working with an agency in Milan, I was asked if I was interested in working in Zürich. I was excited and connected with the Zürich agency by phone. I was directed to come work with them and told that no visa was necessary. So here I am, in the country of my ancestors, and you put me in a jail.*

More questions followed. I focused on the family ties relentlessly, and the judge seemed to let down his guard as a bewildered look crossed his face. He spoke in German to the others in the room and declared that I was to surrender all my vouchers and all the money I had earned from Milan, which they had found in my hotel room. I was denied a work visa for my remaining jobs and placed on a train out of the country.

I thought about calling my agency in Milan, but what were they going to do? I thought about calling Versace, but I was too proud. I thought about calling Kirsten, but I didn't want to get into a discussion about her boyfriend. As we arrived at the train station, I had made up my mind. All I was doing in Europe was running, just like I had in Japan. I'd done everything right in Paris, Milan, and Zürich. I'd shown up on time for everything. I'd worked the scene. I'd wooed clients. I stayed clean. And I'd had enough. I needed to get back to New York and make some money. I knew I had lost traction and momentum, but with a few good paying campaigns, I told myself I would be back on top again. In my own jungle, where I knew all the vines to swing on, no matter how high I was.

At least this time, I was not lying to myself. On the long flight back from Paris, I entertained no thoughts of landing in New York City and staying clean. I did not regale the woman sitting next to me with stories of my escape from a Swiss prison. I did not fall asleep in anyone's coat hoping to start my day in the city refreshed. I landed and immediately returned to the Pleasure Dome and my old life. The clubs. Poppi in East Harlem.

The moment I set foot in Manhattan, I picked up where I left off.

BEGINNING OF THE END

HE HIT HER. THE badass rocker with the sneer dominating the MTV airwaves. I was standing beside him and his female companion in the China Club after-hours—three of us on the edge of the dance floor. The China Club was now my hangout of choice, and I knew the owners, who always placed me in the reserved VIP seating section and gave me carte blanche to stay with a select group after closing.

It was dark, and I heard them arguing. Not sure about what.

And then he hit her. Smacked her right across the face. She winced, grabbed her cheek. She stopped arguing and seemed to suppress a scream.

I looked around. Was I the only one who saw it? No one else was stepping in. No one was looking over and doing the *did-you-see-that* whisper. Was she his girlfriend? A one-night stand? Did she need my help? She didn't try to run, but he had his arm around her now—the same one he hit her with. Was he keeping her from running? Was he holding her up? Was she drunk? Stoned? Coked up like me? I couldn't tell. All I knew was you don't hit women—ever. My dad taught me that.

I'm not saying I had been a saint to women—sex obsession had gone hand in hand with my drug obsession. There were so many attractive women, and I wanted to know them all. Every bit of it was

111

consensual, even if a lot of it wasn't very respectful. Just a few weeks earlier, at the China Club, a woman had confronted me. Said she felt disrespected because I turned her into a one-night stand. She then threatened to hit me in the head with a bottle at the bar. I would've taken the hit if she had connected and never struck back. Because that's not what you do.

But this rock star with the peroxide, shag-style hair just did. VIPs had carte blanche, but not the freedom to do that. Asshole. I didn't even like his music.

My first instinct was to play the hero. Just rush in on the heat of my anger, jump the guy, and beat the shit out of him. Yeah, I was a little rusty from being out of the wrestling room, but despite the cocaine pulsing through me, I still had confidence in my body and my moves. Especially against this guy. This wouldn't be a fight. Clean or coked up, I'd teach him a lesson in less than thirty seconds.

It's strange how much I thought about my dad at that moment. I knew he wouldn't want me fighting. He went into the Marines at seventeen. Fought at Iwo Jima. Never backed down from a problem. You'd think he would be okay if I got into fights to defend my honor or the honor of my friends and teammates. But he told me, no matter what, to never get into a fight. I still did, of course. I was always worried Dad would find out. In high school, guys I knew were getting suspended left and right. After I got in a fight, I always rushed to answer the house phone, just in case someone from the school administration was calling to inform my parents of my misdeeds. They never did.

Later, when I was living on my own at Penn State, I got a little crazier fighting. It happened a lot during the summer, when I was in downtown Washington, DC, with my friends, just to feed my ego and have some fun in front of a crowd. I no longer felt obligated to heed my dad's warnings. I convinced myself it wouldn't reflect badly on my family if I got in trouble. My friends would pick out some muscled-up bully and bait him into challenging me. *I bet you twenty dollars you won't fight that guy over there.* I'd play the drunken, weak-looking guy so he thought it was an unfair fight and wouldn't say no. One night it was a Marine, who was the exact opposite of the honorable man I saw in my dad. We went around the corner, and I didn't even have to hit him. I slid in my mouthpiece—my one piece of protection, my reminder of who I was on the mat—and before he knew what was happening, I picked him up and threw him on his head. Match over.

This wannabe-tough-guy rocker was no Marine, I told myself I would have dad's blessing tonight.

It wouldn't take much to bring this guy down. I took a step toward them. And instantly stopped.

It wasn't my mouthpiece in my pocket anymore. It was cocaine—and a note telling people not to blame themselves when it killed me. My mouthpiece had me prepared, powerful, feeling strong. Wrestling was my drug, and my mouthpiece made me feel in control. Cocaine gave me adrenaline the way wrestling did. But I had no control. Not here. Not now. Not ever.

Worst-case scenarios rushed through my head. *What if I'm brought up on charges and the girl says he never hit her? Who's anyone going to believe? It would be me versus his legal team. All I have is a modeling portfolio, a bunch of old wrestling trophies, and bag of coke in my pocket. If the cops came and found that, I would be the one charged.*

My moral compass was weaker than the bag of cocaine in the pocket of my Levi's. I decided to let the whole thing go. I watched as the rocker and his bruised companion walked up to the front of the dark, nearly empty club. The girl wasn't saying anything. I was a coward. As a wrestler, I never felt this way. I had lost battles, but when I came off the mat, I felt humbled, not humiliated.

I kept watching as people cleared out for the night. I made my way to the door. I looked back a few times, but I had no second thoughts. I didn't wait out on the streets to watch them leave. I simply told the security guy what I saw.

When I tell this story today, people can't believe that I didn't hit him. *Dude, you would've been on Page Six. That would have been the greatest story!*

But they don't understand. I had no options. I had zero control. What I wanted to do—what I knew I could and should do—I couldn't.

A couple of years earlier, Lee Kemp had taught me how a great champion can have many weapons but should never put himself at risk of losing when the stakes are high. That was me now. Only I wasn't strong. I was weak. It didn't matter if my opponent was a notorious asshole and a drunk, or even if he was high like me. It didn't matter if I was stronger, if I had the moves, if I could help, if she did or did not need help. Because I was helpless. I was shackled to the bag in my pocket. In wrestling, if I put the work in, I had control— my opponent only had as much power over me as I allowed. Cocaine was my opponent tonight, not this guy, and I was half a man with the cocaine. Or no man.

I felt hollow again, so I did what I always did. I immediately filled the void with cocaine as soon as I was in a cab heading to the lonely Pleasure Dome. I wasn't motivated to get better; I was motivated to forget.

Alone in my apartment, I put on MTV. "Dancing with Myself" filled the room. I couldn't get away from that guy. I was alone in my painful existence. The same loneliness that overwhelmed me every time I prayed for help, even though I had been shown the signs to find it. The same loneliness that threatened to extinguish the flicker of light and hope inside me. The same loneliness that made me weak.

UN-MODEL BEHAVIOR

AFTER THAT NIGHT IN the club, I gave up attempting to cover my addiction. Ford sent me out for plenty of jobs to sustain my habit, so it didn't seem to affect my work. I didn't wonder if they saw me as an addict, because I didn't care. I had no fear of facing clients in this shape. I had faced opponents ready to rip my head off or break my neck on the wrestling mat. Nothing scared me about showing up wasted in front of a guy with a camera. I didn't care that those moments were being captured and shown to the world. Nobody could really tell. Or I thought they couldn't. Maybe they just couldn't have cared less as long as I did my job. I used to be critically aware of how people perceived me. I'd watch how they looked at my book and then ask for feedback tso I could give them what they wanted. Not anymore.

Even my failures seemed funny to me. When I was chosen as the guy for the new Fruit of the Loom designer underwear campaign, I showed up after partying for three nights in a row. Still, I initially charmed the people at the shoot with stories of a national underwear campaign I did in Japan, where I was superimposed in a woman's hand wearing colorful briefs. Everyone laughed and felt at ease, which was important when doing shots where a model will be virtually naked. I didn't care. I had worn my wrestling singlet in front of thousands of people on any given night, and it left only slightly more to the imagination. All I cared about was that intimate apparel bookings paid a double day rate, plus a national exclusivity buyout fee.

I arrived on the set and was immediately given a manicure. Then the makeup artist applied a full-body toner to enhance my tanned look. The handmade baby blue briefs they handed me were nothing like what would go into the plastic bags at department stores. I put them on and went in front of the lights to shoot as the art director, photographer, and others discussed what I should do and how to tell me in polite terms. I said they should just tell me what they wanted. *Uh…the women of America would like to see the penis outline down and to the left.* I reached in and repositioned, but got body makeup from my arm on the outside of the briefs—just a slight brown makeup mark, but they had to be changed. It looked like exactly what no one wants in or on underwear—a shit stain—and no airbrushing could take it out. *Oops.* I changed and it happened again. *Oops.* Could they tell I was fidgety from the coke? The makeup artist was not going to reach in my pants and make that intimate adjustment in order to cover for me. Thankfully, we managed to complete the shoot on the final pair of underwear.

A few days later, I got booked on a huge job with a top female model to shoot a campaign for fur coats. Once again, I showed up after no sleep, still high from the night before. When my nose began dripping blood on the fur coat, I apologized. But I wasn't sorry. The makeup artist helped me hide what happened.

Little drops of blood on a fur coat, makeup looking like a shit stain. I never saw the perfect analogy for what was happening in my life: signs my addiction was bubbling out from inside me for all to see. I was a shit stain that was becoming a shit storm that was increasingly visible to those around me.

As spring rolled on, the work started to dry up, and I found myself broke again. My New Jersey mafia-connected, strong-arm landlord would show up at my door with veiled threats. *Hey, Johnny*

I don't want any problem. You know what I mean, Johnny? How old are you, Johnny? I don't want any problem, Johnny. You know what I'm trying to say, Johnny? But I knew to stand my ground with this guy. He had three units in our lease-controlled building, which was illegal. I had hired a lawyer, along with the tenants of the other two units in the building, to try and win our leases from him. I was on an official rent strike as the case worked its way through court.

Yet, even if I had not sued my landlord, I still would have been late with my rent. I had poured all I'd earned and some I'd borrowed into my habit. Desperate, I even went so far as to ask Bruce Weber for money. I went to his loft on Watts Street dressed in a camouflage T-shirt and hat, my spring/summer fatigues for heading up to Poppi's in Harlem. Bruce buzzed me up, and when he answered the door, I tried to hide what was going on inside me—the humiliation mixed with my desperation. I felt Bruce's compassion. I was sure he had probably seen this before. I remembered how I respected him at that first shot and how he told me he'd never recommend putting everything into this line of work, how crazy it is, and how he'd encouraged me to stay with my wrestling. The words echoed in my head as he gave me a few American Express Travelers Cheques. I thanked him for everything—everything he had done. As I left to catch the subway, uptown, I told him I'd pay him back someday, and he said, *I believe you, Johnny. I know you will. Take care of yourself.*

But how was I supposed to do that?

The last time I was on a losing streak like this was my freshman year when, after starting the season 8–0, I broke the neck of that strong bull of a man from Cal Poly. I told myself I didn't feel bad, but I felt bad. Then I stayed out with those older guys the night before the next match, and I lost and kept losing. I couldn't hear anything my teammates said to me about getting back on the horse or just focusing on the next match, but at least I was in control, and I was not alone. Now control was the last thing I had. I couldn't listen even when my dad reached out to me.

I hadn't received a letter from my dad that showed his emotions since Japan. This one affected me as deeply. Inside the envelope was a *USA Today* article about another Ford model, who was rehabbing with the help of the head of the Ford Agency. Dad's note reminded me there was an opening in the rehab center near Falls Church that took his insurance, so not to worry that it would cost him or me anything. He said they were worried about me. Just come home.

That my dad would do this for me affected me, but it didn't move me enough to do what he asked. I wrote a letter back filled with lies. *I'm doing this modeling thing and taking advantage of this opportunity. There is nothing getting in the way, and I can do this. I've got everything in perspective. It's all in control. Don't worry about me.* I didn't mention that I'd turned down a grad assistant coaching position at the University of Virginia to pursue this career.

The lies were made worse by the fact that they were a check my body couldn't cash anymore. In the past, drugs never affected me. I could do anything and keep training. In college, I could call up a friend and say, *I'm gonna go on an eight-mile run through the snow. You're the halfway point. Have three bong hits ready for me.* In my first years in New York and Japan and Europe, I still looked the part. But now my body was starting to run down. I was getting thin and losing muscle mass. My cardio was shot. I looked like death warmed over.

And people were noticing, which pissed me off. I started hearing that dreaded phrase I heard from my parents—*I'm worried about you*—everywhere I went. I knew I wasn't in control and they had every right to worry, but their words raked inside of me. Instead of feeling the love, I dug in my heels and got defensive.

Johnny, you have got to take care of yourself.

What do you know? Don't worry about me. Take care of yourself.

Johnny...

Book me. Do your job. Don't project your problems onto me.

Johnny...

I don't need your pity. You aren't really worried about me. You just want to make yourself feel better. Judge not, lest ye be judged, right?

I was saying all these things knowing full well that I had one of my notes in my pocket, in case I died from an overdose. Or died from putting myself in dangerous situations to stay high.

A guy I used to get blow from in DC came for a visit and wanted to purchase a large quantity from my source. In return for the connection, he promised to throw me enough off the top to feed my habit. I immediately went up to Harlem and took a brick out of the Bank of Poppi on credit. Bill went back to DC with his coke, and I had enough to party with for a week. My only job was to bring Poppi's money up the following week via the package Bill would send via overnight courier. I proceeded to go on a brutal binge all over the city.

I woke up a few days later and realized Poppi's package stuffed with thousands of dollars hadn't arrived as scheduled. I called the overnight courier and entered my friend's tracking number at the prompts. The automated response said the package had arrived in Long Island, but that was it. I panicked as I waited for a live representative, and she confirmed that the package had been lost and she didn't have any idea what could have happened to it. *Oh shit.*

I hung up the phone with my heart racing worse than that night in St. Luke's Roosevelt Hospital. Every negative thought raced through my mind. Did the FBI have it, and were they closing in on me to turn on Poppi? Did an employee see the cash through an X-ray and just snatch it, because it was an amount worth risking jail for? Would Poppi come after *me*, thinking I had pocketed the money?

No matter what, I'm dead.

I thought about running, but I had no money to run and no modeling offers to go anywhere. I'd have to literally run, and I'd be dead by the time I got to Jersey. My only chance was to face the music right away. Blurry-eyed and nervous, I hailed a cab with my last funds. Outside, the city was hot as an inferno. *Perfect metaphor,*

I thought. *I'm going to hell.* As we crossed into Spanish Harlem, I saw kids playing in water streaming from a broken fire hydrant, laughing as they quelled the scorching heat. I remembered simpler times as a kid, playing in the sprinkler with my brother and sisters. Things were tense and deadly complicated now.

I told the driver to pull over, paid the fare, and walked the remaining few blocks to Poppi's store. Drenched with sweat, I went to the back and knocked on the two-way mirror. Poppi opened the door. He sounded anxious and angry. *Where you been, mister? You got my money?* I told the truth about the package, and Poppi went ballistic. He unleashed a barrage of obscenities I understood and countless others I didn't. Then he stopped and looked at me, and in a terrifyingly calm voice, he said: *Someone's going to get hurt.*

Poppi continued to interrogate me. He wrote down the tracking number and made some calls in Spanish. I sat for a while wondering if this was it. The phone rang. The person Poppi had checking the tracking gave him the same info that I had gotten about where the package disappeared.

What are we going to do, mister? Someone ripped me off. Someone's going to pay. For some reason, that wasn't me. Poppi believed I wasn't involved. He told me that he'd have a guy investigate it, and I walked away alive.

For now.

I spent weeks wondering if Poppi would change his mind and send a hit man. He never did. But someone else did. Or rather, several someones. My sister Teri reached out at the end of the month and, making no mention of Dad's offer, invited me home. *Why don't you come home for Labor Day and just hang out with us? Get away from all that in the city.* I thought about saying no, but I was tired of fighting. I agreed. How bad could it be?

INTERVENTION

I PACKED MY BATHING suit, my last stash of cocaine, and Jack for my trip home. Jack was a Canadian model and fellow user who had been staying at my apartment, and he invited himself to come down with me. Like everyone those days, he kept saying he was worried about me. I told him he could come on my family escape if he would just shut up. But it wasn't the family holiday I expected. It was an intervention. What a homecoming.

I realized it immediately when I saw everyone sitting in my parents' house. I thought about just turning around and leaving, but I couldn't. We had hitched a ride down with a friend of mine who lived nearby, and she had already left.

So there I stood on a Saturday afternoon, in front of the people I loved most in the world but least wanted any part of right now: my parents, my brother, and three of my four sisters, along with their husbands. My parents immediately made me cringe with their worry mixed with a dose of faith. Prayer was what my parents used to get through hard situations, but my addiction tested their faith, just as Connor's would test my and Kirsten's faith decades later. They could not bear to see their firstborn son shackled by drugs, but my dad trusted me to come through it because of how disciplined I had been with wrestling.

They think they can save me. They think I have control. They think they have time.

Canadian Jack then piped in and made the situation even worse. Jack was a guitar-toting self-promoter and quickly ingratiated himself with my family. As he played the guitar, he actually started singing about the shape I was in and how everyone was worried about me. He sang that I had a big problem. He gave vivid accounts of the Pleasure Dome nights, never revealing that he himself had the same drug problem and was even stealing drugs from me. Yet everyone nodded in appreciation.

You believe this guy over me? He's worse than me. He's crazy.

I stormed off to get high, and the rest of the intervention was postponed until Sunday, when everyone but my parents gathered at my sister's house in nearby McLean. They all confronted me again. My sister Kitty is a prayer warrior, and she told me how my situation was breaking her heart. Then she started to break down. Her husband jumped in for her. An ex-baseball player in the Orioles organization, we always got a kick out of each other. He felt he could talk to me, former athlete to former athlete. He made me get on the scale because he said I looked emaciated. *Do you see yourself? You look real skinny. You're going down the wrong path, and we are all concerned about you.* I dug my heels, but I knew he was right. I shouldn't be anywhere near my fighting weight of 167 pounds, but I was. I used to suck down, cutting twenty pounds of fluids before weigh-ins to get to that weight. Now I sucked down coke.

Right or wrong, I couldn't take any of it. I didn't want their love or help or prayers. I shut down. Refused to talk. When Jack opened his mouth again, I abruptly left the house and made my way back to my parents' house and my old room in the basement. I sat on the sofa and started to finish my bag of coke. Before I did, I called my friend and asked if we could cut our trip short, and when Jack returned, I banished him to another room upstairs. I told him I was kicking him out of the apartment the second we got back to New York.

I looked around the basement bedroom. It was like a shrine to my wrestling past. Trophies. State tournament brackets. Scrapbooks of glory. I could hear my mom pacing around the kitchen above my head. Pacing and praying—that's what she did. Dad prayed. I could feel him doing that too, but none of it was reaching me. They had no idea what to do, whether they should ignore me or just come down. I didn't need their pity or love, but that I could feel it said a lot. My dad grew up believing a tough Irishman doesn't show a lot of emotion. Doesn't hug. Doesn't say *I love you*. Mother was a Swiss-German stoic who believed her actions showed her love. I felt myself calm down, but then their worry (and praying and pacing) above my head had the same effect it had on me in the city. I started getting angry again.

I don't want your worry; I don't need your love. All I need is to get out. I have to get the hell out of here.

As I started to binge in my parent's basement, I didn't write my usual note to stick in my pocket. Instead I wrote a letter. But when I realized I wasn't going to die, my anger started to fade, and the love of the sleeping house washed over me as I wrote.

Donald + Louise
Brought me to this earth
Showed me God's church
That last is sometimes first
Never heard them curse
Loved me at my worst
Let me free to search
Always quenched my thirst
Gave comfort when I hurt
Warned me of life's dirt
Even cleaned my shirts
Made my mind alert

I took off the next morning while my parents were at church. I kept hearing my family's words as I waited for my ride, thinking about how my parents would feel when they read the note and wondered what it meant. I had told them I was leaving from a place of love, but beyond that, what did it mean? Was it a cry for help? An apology? A bigger version of the notes I carried with me all the time? Was it a goodbye? I settled on goodbye.

Actually, it was more of a farewell. They found the letter only after I died.

GOODBYE

IN 1983, AFTER I finished the work for my final photography course, the head of the department invited me to his farmhouse outside of Happy Valley to do my final presentation. He sat drinking a Heineken at the kitchen table while I presented. He critiqued my work, graded me, and with the coursework done, we started talking.

I told him about my cousin Susan, who had been paralyzed in a car crash. He told me he came from a family of healers. He was adamant about helping with her spinal cord injury (my aunt and uncle never took him up on the offer). But he was most interested to hear about Francesco Scavullo and Bruce Weber and the other great photographers I had worked with. He told me he could shoot circles around them technically. I was curious if he could, and hoped maybe we could do a picture worth bolstering my portfolio, so we did some shots out by his barn. While he barked at his dogs, speaking a unique dog language, we tried different poses with different props like a pitchfork. I had no basis to compare my professor's technical ability to Bruce's, but he was out of his element directing me as a model. The shoot was an enjoyable but forgettable experience...

Except for one photograph that I will never forget.

I got an excited call from my professor a few days later. He said something very surprising had happened that blew him away: on a single frame, bolts of light radiated from my core. He told me five of my seven chakras were illuminated. *What?* I didn't know what a chakra was.

He explained that chakra derives from the Sanskrit word for wheel. There are seven chakras that make up a spinning wheel of light in our bodies, which all our spiritual energy flows through. I still had no idea what he meant but knew enough to ask if it could be a light leak in the camera. He said he initially thought the same thing, but he checked and there was nothing. Plus, the possibility of a light leak on that single frame and no other was impossible.

I went to his office at the art department to check out what the big deal was, and I found myself just staring at the picture. As a model shot, it was unremarkable. But those bolts of light? It was exactly as he said: one frame in a hundred had captured rays of brilliant light emanating from me. I had never seen or felt anything like it, and I had no idea what it meant, beyond that it intrigued me as much as it did him. In fact, it intrigued him so much he asked permission to publish it in some new age magazine. I told him that was fine, and it ran in the next issue. Below the photo in the magazine, the caption reads, "The photo uses no special film or technical manipulation. Just something dramatically revealed."

Soon after the picture was published, my professor called me. He said people who saw it were asking him who I was. They said they had to find me. When he told them I was going to New York City to be a fashion model, they had all said, *No!* They had to find me because something terrible was going to happen to me there— people were going to destroy me, destroy that light. I didn't believe it. Even the professor said he found the calls concerning, but he thought I could handle it.

My professor later gave me a copy of the photo. I thanked him and promptly put it with pictures I kept outside my portfolio. I wasn't worried anyone in New York City would see the chakra magazine, but no one was getting that photo from me. I filed it away and figured if it did have some deep meaning, I'd find out someday.

I thought about my professor and the photo on the way back to New York City after my family's intervention. I remembered the words of warning those unknown people sent. They had been right. Something bad had happened, was happening. *Is happening.* I had extinguished that wheel of light in me, replaced it with the drugs that had doused it. I saw that now.

I collapsed as soon as I returned, and then promptly fell deeper into my dependency. I even ended up in the hospital again but told no one. Part of me wanted to be better—to surrender myself and do whatever it took to regain my soul. I would take my dad's offer to pay for rehab. I would find something else, anything—anyone, really.

But who did I have? Loneliness and fear washed over me, and there was only one way I knew to douse those feelings and drown out my family's voices in my head. The drugs preyed on my thoughts. *Hey, John, do you really want your dad to pay for you to get help? He will own your future. You paid your way this far only to be owned by Daddy?*

No, this was it. I would get help. *Come on John*, the powder called from my pocket. *Haven't we been there for you? We made you feel better all this time. Come on, what's one last binge between friends? You can wait one more day, right?*

I grabbed my keys and headed out. And for the first time since I could remember, I didn't write a note before I left.

◆◆◆

I NODDED AT THE doorman as I walked past the line at Studio 54 and made straight for the bar. I ordered a Heineken and surveyed the main floor. I took a walk through every corner of the club that I knew so well, looking for a girl that I might invite home with me to share my farewell to the Pleasure Dome. I ended up going to the old theater seat section on the top floor, where I got high alone. The music was pulsating. *Tainted love. I've got to get away from the pain...and I've lost my light. Take my tears and that's not nearly all!* How appropriate.

After the first high started to wear off, I made up my mind to go home.

As I dragged myself along the streets of my Hell's Kitchen neighborhood, I never felt lower. The fall air was clear and crisp, but I kept my hands in my jacket pocket—not for warmth, but so anyone considering mugging me would think twice about what I might be holding. The cool air cleared my mind a bit. *No more*, I thought. *I will find help. I will flush the remaining drugs down the toilet, make that painful transition from high to sleep, and call my dad in the morning.* But was I serious about getting help, or was I just saying the words that would get me to my next supply of drugs? The only thing; the most important thing. That next hit. The next time.

As I approached my building, I didn't believe anything I said one way or another, and I found myself doing something I had not done since sitting in the Italian church: I prayed for help. That's when I saw Joel from across the hall, in his socks, buzzing my apartment door. He had never been inside the Pleasure Dome, and I had never spoken to him before, but he knew what went on in there and had observed in me what I had in him: all the hallmarks of a fellow addict. Aside from that, I knew two other things about Joel, only the second of which was important to me at all, but especially tonight: he was gay, and he was a psychiatrist with a private practice.

Maybe Joel was the answer to my prayers. God was putting me in touch with a psychiatrist to get help. Joel saw me and stopped buzzing. *You're a doctor, right, an MD?* Joel nodded. I told him my deal. I said I needed to speak to him about some medical questions and drug treatment. That I really needed to see a doctor, and maybe he could help me or point me in the right direction to get help. If so, I had an offer for him.

Joel sized me up. I've had girls and guys check me out before. I know what it feels like. I told him I was not gay or interested in that, so anything sexual was not an option. But… *You're high on coke and desperate for more, right? So am I. I have a pure bag from my*

Colombian friend in Harlem. After I get rid of it, I want to check into rehab. Help me, and I'll help you.

Joel agreed, and we entered his apartment. He went through all his doctor motions in good faith: checked me out, took my blood pressure, and listened to my chest with a stethoscope. As he did, he answered my questions about my fear of dying on coke. Said they were legitimate and that he would help me. I believed him. I gave him my bag of coke.

Then he pulled out a box of little orange-tipped syringes.

I recoiled a little. Despite the kilos of cocaine I had ingested, I'd still only injected cocaine that one time as a teenager. I was so freaked out by it, I never tried it again. But I sold myself on the fact that Joel was a doctor, and from the marks on his arms, he'd clearly done this many times. *If this is going to get me help, that's what I'm going to do.*

Joel prepped the syringe and shot himself in the vein on his hand. He then prepped a new syringe and gave me an injection just below my right bicep. With the first beat of my heart, I felt the drug rush straight through my body and tasted it immediately. It was the same intense high I remembered from years before.

That's when Joel started questioning me about wrestling, and then taunting me about it. He said he was a big fan of professional wrestling. I let him know that was stupid and fake. *Oh yeah? Wrestle me! Show me a move.* Joel was in my face now, hands on me. I knew what to do. Before he could react, I picked him up in a fireman's carry, gave him a spin, and threw him down on the ground. *That's real wrestling.*

I was ready for Joel to keep the rest of his promise, but he was all hyped up. He smiled and bounced up and said, *Let's do one more! Come on, one more tonight!* I said no. I had to get home and get some help. He insisted. *One more. One more.* And just like I had when those cool kids pressured me into smoking marijuana on the railroad ties behind the pool in Falls Church, I caved.

Okay. Joel pulled out two new syringes. *This is going to get me to help.* He prepared the coke. *Point me in the right direction.* He injected himself. *One last time, my last hurrah, this is all just a means to an end.* He injected my bicep again.

It wasn't anything like the drug I knew, or anything like the shot I had fifteen minutes earlier. Cocaine goes through you instantly. You feel it on your tongue. You feel it everywhere as it takes you higher. As soon as the needle plunged into me, I felt the exact opposite of high. I could feel my body shutting down. The power was beyond anything I had ever felt before. My body had hit its limit.

This is the end—this is death, what the last moments of life feel like. An anguish and a pain beyond anything I had ever known filled me.

COULD NOT HOLD ON

I FELL FACE DOWN on the floor. Then I felt my legs being pulled up. But it wasn't Joel. No one was lifting my legs off the floor. Instead, I felt my legs being pulled out of my body by some unseen force. I was drowning in a sea of darkness, but my instinct was to fight. Every part of me was consumed with something beyond fear: that if I let go, this would be my last moment on this earth. My grip was slipping, the finality of my flesh and bones losing life. There was pain and unspeakable turmoil as I struggled in a dark abyss against what felt like the strength of three, four powerful men pulling at my legs and ankles, pulling me right out of my body, upward and outward. I reached for my waist with a torso grip. *Hold on, John!* But the force was overwhelming, tremendous. I couldn't hold on. My grip broke. I was ripped free from my body.

This was pure petrified darkness. Worse than any horrifying thing I had ever imagined. This was NOT the answer to my prayers. This was what it felt like to die.

◆◆◆

I WAS WHISKED INTO further darkness, but soon arrived at a place of light and pain-free solitude. I found myself standing, and I could breathe again, a new breath of life that radiated through me. Simultaneously, I could see Joel's apartment—Joel freaking out, listening to my chest, starting repetitions for CPR, trying to revive me. As he did, I felt a growing part of me realize I didn't want him to bring me back. I didn't care to be in that body, now that my soul stood radiant in a new light. My fear had been replaced with complete fulfillment. The pain was gone.

Then I stood before the brightest illumination imaginable, a radiance beyond description. More of a piercing brilliance than a glow—a feeling of pure truth and love that now embraced me. My last bit of fear disappeared, and so did the apartment. I had arrived in a new place—a space filled with that amazing light that was more than a light. Beautiful doesn't begin to describe it. It filled me with all the answers, and I realized the voice I heard had always been with me, but muted. If Heaven is a contentment that every soul yearns to feel, I was in Heaven. The light I basked in was clearly the source of my existence—my Creator. And it wasn't just coming from around me… it was *in* me. I was in the light. I was of the light. I became one with it.

The light was truth. The light was love—love that is in and flows through and between all of us. The light that connects us. The light that my professor captured in one photo and then I had extinguished, imprisoned, cluttered, and blocked with my ego and addiction. I was now home, sharing in the fulfillment of truth and love. I knew I was where every soul on Earth somehow yearned to be, was meant to be, suffered to be. My feeling was one of love for all, and my hope was for all souls to return to this light of fulfillment.

I had jammed its frequency during my life. Now, I not only felt it, I heard it; a rush or rambling filled my ears. Through it all, I felt the prayers of love from my family and everyone who had prayed for me, especially my parents and my sister Teri, who had wanted me to get help. I didn't feel like I was being judged. I just felt like I was being loved, and the love of those people reflected in the source of the light around me. I now saw their prayers as solid objects. My father and mother's prayers were the strongest, their many hours of prayer standing tall like solid pillars in the light. My sister Teri's prayers were a smattering of stones beneath my feet, holding me up. The smaller stones of my brother and other sisters' prayers joined hers.

I reached out to touch the pillars, but they dissipated into vibrational energy. I tried to call to all of them—to tell them where I was, but the words wouldn't come out. I focused on what I wanted to say to them through this fountain of light. What was my truth? What I really wanted was to ask the light—the source of truth and love—that those people I loved and everyone I left behind not be made to suffer. That they know my soul was alive and fulfilled.

I couldn't speak, but I quickly learned to let a new language of light flow through me. I laughed at my frustration. At last single words started to come out haltingly. I spoke to my Creator.

Please…Please don't…Please don't let my parents blame themselves.

I felt calm. The words begin to flow more easily, like the notes I left behind most nights. Like the note I failed to leave on my physical body tonight.

Please don't let Joel's life be ruined by having to explain my dead body on his floor.

Please comfort my family and let them realize I am okay now. I know where I am. I am where I am meant to be. I am with You. My thirst is quenched. I am where we all long to be.

I wish everyone I love will spend the rest of their days not in mourning or regret but in peace of heart. Don't block out the joy of this light with feelings of suffering, loss, blame, or failure for my departure from your realm.

I repeated words like these over and over, as the light reflected their prayers and concerns back to me.

I don't know how much time went by. I don't know if time even existed.

I let this frequency keep filling me with a presence I had dulled with the dark despair of drugs. I was where I was meant to be—where all of us are meant to be. Where the earthly void is filled not by ego-satisfying conquests and the cheers of the crowd, but by pure love. I laughed and marveled at the beauty. My soul was radiant.

As I let more and more of it in, I was shown my life. I was shown it all forward and backward in the same instant, filling the infinite space. My ears and eyes filled with everything from birth to that moment on Joel's floor—all the pain and hurt, joy and love. Little things, big things, triumphs on the mat, tragedy chasing the drugs—every emotion washed over me.

I wept as I saw myself born in 1960 and met my mother's eyes for the first time, screaming until the warmth of her body filled me with love from the outside the way she had when I was inside her. The nurses buzzed around me, insisting that I be named George because we were in Washington, DC, and it was George Washington's birthday. My mother laughed and said my name was John, which means *gift*, as it was also her birthday and I was her gift: her first boy.

But when I looked at the end, my soul torn from my body, I felt the force on my legs happening all over again. Only this time it felt different—like I was being pushed, not pulled. Or rather, pulled back. I could still feel the light, it was still with me—but now the only light I saw was from the ceiling in Joel's apartment. I was not in that infinite dimension anymore. I was not hovering over my body. Joel's body was now hovering over me.

◆◆◆

STARTLED, I JUMPED UP and back, onto the sofa. I patted my legs and arms. Joel stared at me. He didn't say anything. Whether his silence was from shock that the body he had given up on was suddenly sitting up on his sofa, or relief that he did not have to explain a dead body in his home, or the drugs were overtaking his rush of adrenaline, I did not know.

Joel gave me that *Dude, what the hell?* look. I told him what I had experienced and where I had been. I told him I'd seen him give up on reviving me and frantically run around his apartment, throwing the needles and coke in the incinerator chute, and then return to try again. A psychiatrist, he brushed it all off as a psychological phenomenon. I tried again. A doctor, he said that wasn't possible, even though I had been dead on his floor. I tried one more time to explain, but none of my words did the light justice.

I stood up to leave. The sun was up, and I realized I felt no residual effects from the drug. There was absolutely no hint of the three days of toxic-level drugs that nearly took my life. My mind was clear and sober. In place of the high, I felt the light. I had brought the light I had lost and then found again back with me to this realm.

I crossed the hall to my apartment. The sun was streaming in the window and bouncing off the giant mirror on the wall. Its rays shining in the dust reminded me of my chakra picture. I dropped to my knees and repeated the same two words over and over. *Thank you, thank you, thank you…* Then more words. *Thank you, God, for letting me back in.*

My return was a second chance at life with that light inside me. My return was the only way my loved ones would not suffer the anguish of losing me. My return was the only answer to fulfill the request I made to my Creator.

I don't know why I got to come back. I don't know why I get to try and make sense of this connection, but I know I have to. I looked out the window at the stream of people on the sidewalk heading to work. I vowed to make sure they and everyone I loved and met knew that. I felt a connection to every soul on Earth in a way I never had before. I would share and reflect this source of love with the world and help them recognize what I'd seen: the frequency of truth and love within each of them. This was my purpose—I just knew it. It was awe-inspiring.

So, I let it out. I told my story to everyone I met. I learned quickly that Joel's dismissal of my experience was not the exception. Malone just laughed and told me, *John, God doesn't come to you when you're on drugs.* They and everyone else shut me down. Desperate to find anyone who would listen, I tracked down an actor who had been pronounced dead in a swimming accident. He had told his story on *The Tonight Show* to Johnny Carson, but he had nothing to share, except his desire for a date with me.

Before I died, I had felt disconnected and alone. Now I felt connected to everything and yet more alone than ever. People looked at me like I used to look at this guy at Penn State who preached about salvation. He would stand on the steps in front of the Willard building and bellow about Jesus and how we were all sinners. Almost everyone regarded him as a curiosity, not a messenger. Was that what I had become? *How can I describe this to people? How can I have an influence on people? Why did I get to come back? I've got to be a messenger!*

I felt the risk of losing the light.

When my roommate Susie came home and saw me, she knew immediately that something was wrong. She could tell this wasn't about the addiction and asked to know as much as possible. I told her. She didn't tell me to stop talking either. She believed me. Told me I was lucky. And for the first time in days, I felt some peace.

A couple of days later, Susie saw the frustration filling me again and offered an escape: a road trip to her family's farm in Pennsylvania. I decided I had to leave the city. I just couldn't focus there, but I wasn't ready to go home yet and try to share what I had been through with my family. I accepted Susie's offer.

The first morning at the farm, I walked over to the barn alone. As I looked over the landscape, I sat in the mantra position I had learned in Tokyo, legs crossed on top of each other, hands on each knee, palms pointed up. I start to meditate. Not that I knew anything about meditating, but I knew where I wanted to put myself. I looked up at the sky and thought about the light until I could feel it coming into me again. I was still connected to it. I smiled.

That's when I started seeing squiggly streaks and tight little spheres of light dancing around in the sky. I still see them today. Tears dripped down my cheeks. I didn't want to stand up, fearing

I'd lose them and their energy, but I had to trust that I could find them again. The next day, they were still there in the sky, and around Susie and her family too. I didn't understand what they were or why they followed me. It dawned on me that my photography professor, who took that picture and taught me about chakras, might be able to help.

I called him and described what I'd seen. I could practically hear his smile over the phone. He told me the energy was prana; it was part of my own connected energy. Like chakra, prana comes from Sanskrit, and it refers to the life force that connects all the elements in the universe. He said I wasn't seeing it with my eyes; I was recognizing it. He reminded me of the photo, how the light came from me, and said I must have learned to keep that light with me.

This is a gift, John, he said.

♦♦♦

A GIFT, FOR SURE, but still a curse. I wanted to convey my message to others—that their prayers of love could hold those they loved in the light and give them strength. But if I had struggled to connect with anyone about the truth and love I saw in my death experience, explaining the energy I now saw dancing around them only made it harder. My parents wanted to believe me but struggled to understand what I had gone though. I thanked them for their prayers but refused their offer to go into rehab one more time. I understood that a twelve-step recovery program was aimed at beginning to understand how we answer to a higher power. But I had already been immersed in the full light of that higher power. No rehab could make me feel better or give me more insight into the essence of my higher power.

So I did exactly what my ego made me do when my family intervened, what I had been shown not to do: I shut them out and made my way back to New York City. As I walked the streets, the prana danced alongside me. Soon, however, I noticed a dark shadowy energy trying to gain my focus.

At first, I managed to keep it at bay. I had control for about a month. But my frustration with others and their inability to hear my story was growing. I blamed them for their failure to be receptive when I should have blamed myself. Why would I expect them to be receptive? Why would Malone or anyone who knew me before suddenly open up to my experience? They hadn't been in the light. They were in the exact same place they had always been. I couldn't even remember what bullshit Malone and I talked about before my near-death experience. Now I expected them to go this deep with me? The days became one long self-immolation.

Come on, John. Who are you kidding? You're not fixed. You may feel this. You may know this is your quest. But you haven't let others in. You're telling them what you know, and yet you have no idea what it means to share it. This is all the same bullshit as before: conquest and control. John dominating like he did on the mat. Like he did in front of the camera. No one has heart-to-hearts with you. No one knows how much it hurt you to leave wrestling. No one understands that you didn't know how to stop the drugs—that you still don't know. You haven't exactly been receptive to others. Receptive to help. Receptive to the intervention of your family. You weren't even freaking receptive to the near-death experience. No, you did what you always do: you ran away. You're still running away. You're hiding the drug use that sent you to the light. You focus on the saint and whitewash the sinner. People aren't receptive because the story is coming from a John nobody knew—it's coming from a John that never existed. Still doesn't exist. Because he's still hiding. Because he's still lying to himself.

It was the end of October, and I had been off of drugs for more than a month, doing some modeling, when I couldn't take it anymore. The shadowy energy was back. There were no more words to help me explain, but there was cocaine to help me forget. I took my payday from the few gigs I had, went by my apartment, changed into my Army jacket, and headed up to East Harlem. I walked through the market and knocked on the glass window. Poppi opened the door.

Hey, mister, where have you been? I haven't seen you in a long time. Where's that cocksucker friend of yours? He owes me money. You tell him I'm going to kill him.

I told him I hadn't seen my friend, but I had money for what I needed. Poppi smiled, laid out a few lines for the road, and handed me a sandwich-size Ziploc with enough cocaine to kill my pain for weeks. I hailed a gypsy cab and jumped in the back of the sedan's crushed velvet seats. The cab was fragrant with rearview mirror air freshener, and I nearly gagged as I snorted some more cocaine in the backseat. I saw the driver's eyes looking back at me. I just snorted more coke and stared back.

I hated myself for being so weak. I had been in the ultimate source of truth and love, but every time I thought about not having the words to describe it, I felt more frustration. Which only made me want to get high and escape. I got out at the China Club and finally went back home around 5:00 a.m. I couldn't sleep. I knew I would be up for days as I finished the bag.

For the first time since before my death, I wrote a note and put it in my pocket.

◆◆◆

EVERYTHING WAS STILL MORNING quiet when I heard heavy footsteps in the hallway. I didn't hear a knock, but I still quietly walked to the front door and looked out the peephole. My heart raced at the sight of a gold-plated NYC detective badge across from my door. *They're coming for me! And I've got enough cocaine in my apartment to keep me up for three more days!*

I rushed back into my apartment on my tiptoes, grabbed the cocaine and the little grinder I used to break up the rock, and headed into the bathroom. I emptied the baggie into the toilet and flushed. I then flushed the baggie with everything else. I rinsed the grinder and wiped it out with a towel. I was taking it back to the kitchen when I heard pounding on the door. I didn't even have time to put on a shirt.

The detective flanked by uniform cops stood in the hall. He said he'd like to ask me a few questions and could he come in. I played it cool, even though he could probably see the drugs in my face. I let him in. *What happened? What's the problem?* He didn't answer my questions as he looked around my apartment, empty beer bottles on a table next to a box of overflowing jewelry. He looked at the box suspiciously. I told him my roommate was a jewelry designer and showed him her ad in *Details* magazine, which happened to be open on the table. He looked down, and then up at me.

Did you hear any unusual noises last night? I told him no, I got home around 5:00 a.m. but hadn't heard any noises until he knocked on my door. *What happened?* Again he wouldn't say. He just looked at my ID, recorded my name, birth date, and contact info. *Thank you, we may be back with follow up questions.* For what? I had no idea. All I knew was I just flushed a bag of coke for no reason. I was both curious and angry. About twenty minutes later, another knock at the door; I figured it was the cops with more questions. But when I opened the door, a bright light filled my eyes and I could not see.

For a moment I was reminded of the light I had betrayed, that I had dimmed again. Then my eyes focused: a microphone with a bright orange foam tip, held in the grip of a reporter. The light was attached to a camera held by a cameraman. A news crew. I heard the reporter's questions for the first time. *Sir, sir, do you know anything about the murder across the hall?*

Joel was murdered? No, it was the other way around, I soon realized: Joel had committed a homicide and would be charged with second-degree murder of a male companion he had strangled with a cable cord. *Do you know anything about it? About the psychiatrist being charged?*

I focused. I realized this wasn't live TV. I was a model; I knew how to show up in front of a camera. I told them to turn off the camera. *You are putting a package together, and I can answer your questions and give you something better if you just wait.* I closed the door.

I rinsed my face, wet and finger combed my hair, and put on a shirt. Then I let the crew inside and told them to wait while I went next door to get my neighbor, an actress on *Search for Tomorrow*. I brought her over, and the two of us sat on the sofa in front of my black table, positioning ourselves in front of the beer bottles to hide them.

The reporter asked his questions, and we gave them the neighbors' reactions. They thanked us and left, telling us the story would run on the evening news. And just like that, within an hour, everyone was gone: the TV crew, the police, my neighbor Joel, and the young man who was his victim, carried out in a well-worn black body bag and placed in a dented blue and gold van with Morgue written on the back. Just the way I thought my body would be pulled out of there a month before.

I had seen the light again, but in the strangest of ways: in Joel's victim's body. A dead man shown his life once and now a dead man showing him what could have been. This was my God wink: a seemingly coincidental experience so crazy, no one would believe it was anything but divine intervention.

I swore right then never to be so alone. I didn't know how to do that, but I would get there. I would find my path and learn to tell my story about being in the source of truth and light, to share it with others. *It has to be about sharing the love I was shown. That's how I was able to speak in the light.* Relationships are not one way. Love is not one way. This was not about needing the cheers of the crowd. It was not about a conquest. There was nothing wrong with a little ego and using my skills to deliver a great performance, but I had to do it openly and truthfully if I was ever going to fulfill my quest.

I had to let others into my life and truth. I needed to go through in life what I did in my death: a rebirth.

Doing that meant I had to admit how and why I died. I had to be the living version of the notes I had written in case I overdosed. That was not going to be easy. That was going to take time and luck and a little fate. What it was not going to take was cocaine. That was going to be hard. Accepting the unknown was not something I had ever done well, but I did not want to be in that body bag anytime soon.

Later that evening, the story about Joel aired on the news, and I decided to leave my apartment a few hours later. Out on Fifty-Seventh Street, the crazy old lady from the neighborhood noticed me. *I saw you on TV. Nice place you got up there.* I smiled and nodded my thanks.

I took a long walk downtown and passed a church with an opaque glass door. I heard beautiful voices in song vibrating from the other side. I opened the door. A celebration of radiant souls, singing and swaying and dancing down the aisles, filled my eyes and ears with joy. The preacher wore flowing purple robes and sounded out a message of love. A woman in a blue dress with a ruffled collar and matching blue hat turned my way and waved me in. She and the others greeted me with hugs and smiles. Their energy pulled me into their celebration. I prayed with them. I felt them and I knew. I knew what I needed the love and strength for: I needed to find a way to make sure others felt the light too, so they didn't experience death before their time. One less body bag. I felt humbled by the thought, something I had not felt in a long time. I felt hope—hope that I could overcome my loneliness and learn to deliver the message I was meant to deliver no matter how long it took. Even if I did not know how or when I would have the strength—even if it took baby steps—I would find redemption.

Revived, I headed back uptown. I made no profound resolutions. I knew I was still broken. Incomplete. But destined to do more.

Back in my apartment, the phone was ringing. It was my aunt, who saw the news and was calling me excitedly from Sag Harbor. *What's going on up there, angel? We saw you on the news. That guy was crazy—so sorry you had to go through that. You need to come out here? You know you're always welcome.*

I was emptying my drugless pockets on the table as she spoke, and I saw the note I'd written the night before. I looked at it and did make one resolution that night before throwing it away: it would be the last note I ever wrote.

My aunt was still talking to me. *Angel, are you okay?*

Yeah, I'm okay, I say.

And for the first time since I started using, I meant it.

My "Portrait of a Wrestler" feature for L'uomo Vogue *shot by Bruce Weber/NYC, 1982*

1981 NCAA Championships. Winning the consolation finals match over Iowa State's Perry Hummel (5–4). (Photograph by Janis Burger)

God's-eye view image of my final Rec Hall Dual Meet match (2/18/82), beating Gibble 11–1 (Photograph by B. Gammerman)

Representing Team USA vs USSR. Ready to meet and do battle with my Soviet World medalist opponent. (L–R: Bill and Jim Scherr, me, Lou Sondgeroth)

Winning my second EWL Conference Championship and simultaneously getting my 100th career victory (2/27/82) (Photograph by Marshall Goldstein)

Gracing the cover of MGF magazine's June 1985 edition.

(Photograph by Christopher Makos)

躍動感の
エレガントなリファイン

撮影・半川也寸志
スタイリスト・松村美幸　ヘア＆メイク・山田公／JET　モデル・リディア・ション

ゴーメンゴールの
スポーツ感覚かこの秋
あなたをリんくＯ！

*I appeared in Marie Clare magazine wearing various sports uniforms, seen here in a uniform
I was very familiar with. (Photograph by Yashushi Handa/Tokyo)*

I made the cover of Menswear *magazine on my second New York City shoot.*
(Photograph by Albert Bray/NYC)

Me as the face of the international Versace campaign 1984.
(Photograph by Bruce Weber/NYC)

Dancing on my toes in an ad for the designer campaign, Domon.
(Photograph by Yasushi Handa/Tokyo)

Typical day on the set with a couple female supermodels.
(Photograph by Stan Malinowki/NYC)

My polaroid from a Swiss TV magazine cover shoot. An hour later I was locked up in a Zürch jail cell as an undocumented immigrant

My beautiful wife, Kirsten.
(Photograph by Paco Navarro/Spain)

Pajamas take a walk. Outdoors that is! Long-sleeved pajama top with vertical blue and white stripes, full placket with covered buttons, about $50, by Tous Les Calecons. White shorts with elastic waist and ribbed cotton, about $25, also by Tous Les Calecons.

Men's Guide to Fashion *magazine editorial shoot in New York.*

(Photograph by Knut Bry)

The day I married Kirsten in Sag Harbor, NY. Photograph by Bruce Weber, who had introduced us on a Vogue shoot in Las Vegas

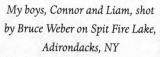

My boys, Connor and Liam, shot by Bruce Weber on Spit Fire Lake, Adirondacks, NY

With my boys: Liam, my nephew Sean, and Connor in Miami Beach, FL
(Photograph by Scott Teitler)

JOHN HANRAHAN,
PRIVATE TRAINER

"For $95 an hour, I impose a series of stresses on
your body so the body becomes better able to
handle the stresses of daily life," says Hanrahan,
a former U.S. team wrestler and a trainer of
Hollywood moguls, professional athletes and regular
couch potatoes. Cotton-and-spandex tank top by
Calvin Klein Underwear, $27. Cotton drawstring
judo pants by Nova USA, $75. Shoes by Nike, $60.

Featured in GQ magazine as "the guy you should know for fitness"
(Photograph by Timothy Greefield Sanders/NYC)

*With my son Connor after receiving my 1996 Olympic Trials
medal earned at the Brockport, NY event*

*On top of the UWW World Championship podium winning the Gold medal
in Walbrych Poland 2016*

PENNSYLVANIA
WRESTLING ROUND-UP

JUNE 2016

The Timeless Wonder at 57!
Former Penn State All-American
John Hanrahan

Magazine Devoted
Exclusively to Wrestling
in the Keystone State

Vol. 35 No. 6

Featured on the cover of Pennsylvania Wrestling Round-Up.
Top image: Defeating my opponent from Turkey at the 2015 UWW Championships in Athens,
Greece (by Dan Studenik). Bottom image: Winning both the Greco-Roman and Freestyle Master's
National Championships at the US Open in Las Vegas, 2016 (by Eric Cluck)

PART II
REFLECT THE LIGHT

Call LEG-ORUB

I *WAS OKAY IN* the days after the detectives and body bag shook me out of my relapse, but I knew I had only taken the first steps. I was not clean. I was not free. I could feel the temptation from withdrawal, and I knew I hadn't broken my weakness for cocaine. I was still an addict, still struggling to explain my experience and the lights I saw every day around others. Cocaine was a snake and it was everywhere in this jungle, calling me to take a bite of its powdery apple. How easy would it be to forget this light, run up to Poppi in Harlem, and swing open the doors of the Pleasure Dome? But I would never return to Harlem again.

Relapse might be part of recovery, as they say, but I had no interest in falling this fast. I needed to do something. Rehab was the best option. But pride was still in my way. Going home made me feel like a loser, and I needed to feel like a winner again.

So I did what I always did: I ran. Only this time, I ran back rather than away.

The last time I'd visited Penn State, a feature article on me ran in the *Centre Daily Times* newspaper about how I had "dropped" wrestling, left my record-setting career on the mat in Happy Valley behind, and parlayed that success into a glamorous career as a world-class model. But I never dropped wrestling for modeling.

I dropped wrestling because the drugs made me believe I could not win anymore. Yet it was still part of who I was. When I was holding onto my life, the one thing I knew was that I was a wrestler. Wrestlers fight for their lives. It was cool to see myself in pictures and advertisements all over the place. It certainly helped me get the girls I wanted. But I didn't have to fight for any of that. There was still a fighter inside me, and modeling did not offer me the control wrestling did. Modeling was a means to an end—almost literally my end from a cocaine overdose. The last time I truly had a winning mindset was as a wrestler. Maybe there was still some mojo at Penn State. After all, it was where I had dug myself out of the biggest losing streak of my life, when I lost five matches in a row freshman year.

Still, I hadn't showed up for anything wrestling-related since I quit the New York Athletic Club. On top of that, I had let down Coach Lorenzo and my dad by finishing two courses short of my degree when my career as a model/addict started taking too much of my time in my fifth year. It was very important to Coach that everybody who wrestled for him graduate: *Great wrestlers at Penn State get a great education*, he always said. Maybe I could still fulfill his wish.

I called down to Penn State, not to Coach—who I had let down again by not showing up to my Hall of Fame induction—but to a couple of the guys I used to mentor as a senior and grad assistant. They were the grad assistants now. They invited me to stay at their apartment, no questions asked. I grabbed some clothes and headed to Port Authority to catch a bus. Despite missing the Eastern Wrestling Hall of Fame induction and losing my last match at the NYAC tournament finals before walking away from the sport, my reputation in Rec Hall was sturdy.

If my reputation was tarnished with Coach Lorenzo, he did not let me know. Papa Bear was a forgiving man and welcomed me to workout with the team. He said he knew I was still two courses short of getting my degree and was happy I would keep my promise to him. Not knowing exactly how long I would be there, I registered for the missing classes—a math class and a Spanish class—as correspondence courses.

Working out at Penn State with the team was immediately grounding and humbling. Back in the wrestling room, I looked at the wall where I always pictured my National Champion portrait would hang—something I visualized every grueling practice for four years. I remained proud that I had never once missed a single practice or match due to illness, injury, or addiction. I found myself among the smaller All-American pictures that ring the room below the giant National Champion portraits. I had every opportunity to place my face there and came up short. But putting on my Nittany Lion fatigues of blue shorts and a gray T-shirt, getting on my gear, going into the room, and actually wrestling took away the pain—by giving me a big dose of it.

Any wrestling dreams that still lived inside me were pure fantasy in my current shape. On a scale of one to ten, I was a 1.1. So I went at it hard. I didn't wrestle great, but I kept going, taking on three, four, five guys in a row. Over and over again, icing myself down, working out, bulking up, and facing this young group of elite wrestlers. They all knew who I was and asked me to tell the stories that had been passed down like folklore. They all knew what they needed and I needed. They all relished the chance to take me down to build them—and me—up. I was thanking God for the opportunity to get my ass kicked, rekindle my fighting spirit, and test my fortitude. To remind myself that there was light in this darkness.

I never once thought about drugs even as I took my poundings. Instead of trying to tell Coach or any of the wrestlers about my experience and the lights all around us, I started writing new notes—powerful, spiritual notes—to remind me of what I'd witnessed:

> Dear Light of the World, O Lord we hunger for Your love—
> we stray far from Your banquet of eternal fulfillment. We
> fill these intense appetites with earthly desires, which only

creates more emptiness, further away from Your banquet of eternal life and fulfillment. Your Light gives us hope, Your loving spirit strengthens our direction. Other souls reflect Your light and give us inspiration—teach us patience, prudence, and discipline. Thank You for this challenging journey of hope. You have set us free through Your pure love. Our selfishness has led us astray and has created this painful distance from Your light of peace and tranquility. Thank You, Lord. We need only to share Your loving grace with those around us. We are all unworthy, yet we have been given hope and strength through Your Light. Your spirit is here and strengthens us along Your path of salvation. Thank You, Lord. We have many gifts from You, yet we abuse them through our blindness. We beg forgiveness again and again. We long to serve You and once again be worthy of Your all-fulfilling Love.

My grip on things was returning. But I knew it was tenuous. Not just because there were drugs in Happy Valley and I still knew who to contact, but also because this wasn't reality. There was no going back to college. No reclaiming any lost years. And New York City was a short drive away. My agency knew where I was. I had told them where to reach me so no one would think I died or filed a missing person's report. I needed the money from a big job, but what would I do with it when I got it?

Three weeks into my Penn State rehabilitation, Ford indeed called and told me a high-paying client wanted me for a job. I hesitated but decided to face my fears, and my need for cash, and head back to the city for the job.

There would be no job.

I showed up at the client's on time the next morning and they sent me away saying I looked overweight. Before they did, they snapped Polaroids of me and sent them over to my booker via messenger with the note: *Too chubby*. Just months before, I had been too thin for my family. I had certainly bulked up and gained weight since the drugs left my system and I began working out at Penn State. But...*chubby*? How dare they judge me like that? No one had ever taken a job away from me before. Did they want me to look like the coked-out rail-thin models and become part of what was then called Heroin Chic?

I returned to the Ford offices and talked to the head booker at Ford. She tried to comfort me. As she spoke, I saw my magazine covers hanging on the wall behind her with all the top cover models in the men's division. But unlike my picture at Penn State, that picture could and probably would come down after today. I just didn't have the sense that she was going to push me for work anymore. I was done.

I was angry. I was humiliated. I was me in third grade after I lost my first wrestling match ever. A loser—a loser who yearned for a high. Harlem beckoned me, but I managed to resist. I slunk back to Penn State, but I didn't head back to the wrestling room. I didn't look the part of wrestler, model, or addict anymore. What was I? Who was I? *I can't win in wrestling or modeling in the big city. I'm out.*

So I took off. Only this time, I ran into the arms of my family—specifically my sister Teri in Chicago.

Modeling was the best way I knew to make money, but I needed jobs that weren't looking for drug-addled models. Chicago was the perfect choice: I had an agency contact there, and the city didn't follow New York's lead when it came to Heroin Chic. If Teri would welcome me, I felt sure I could get back on my feet in that market. She had moved out there with her husband, who was a producer for ABC and had a fellowship at the University of Chicago. They offered me sanctuary in the guest room of their apartment in exchange for helping take care of their kids when I wasn't working.

I had enough money for the plane fare. I took my book to my new agent at Elite Chicago. The whole office was delighted to have my not-too-chubby-for-Chicago body. There was not a lot of work to be had at the moment, but I got a couple of big jobs for department stores, a national Harley Davidson campaign, and some smaller gigs.

Chicago was a nice change of pace from New York City—for a while. I built up some funds and stayed off the streets except for dates with the pretty agency receptionist. Every night, I came home to my sister's family and felt their love. I stayed about two months, until I felt I'd overstayed my welcome in my sister's guest room. At least, that was the story I told myself. Truth is, life was too slow in Chicago. It wasn't stimulating. Even the big jobs were little jobs for someone like me. It was beneath me. Second tier. It pissed me off. *This isn't what I do. I'm freaking John "the Hammer" Hanrahan.*

But I didn't know where to go next. This was not how my rebirth was supposed to be. I didn't know what I needed, so I went to my place of last resort—or first resort. I called my parents and told them I was coming home to Falls Church to lay low and find my way. Mom said she would have the basement ready for me.

If I was going to be reborn a winner, it was going to be where it all started. I surrendered to the idea.

◆◆◆

MY PARENTS DIDN'T REALLY talk to me. They did what they usually did: they prayed while my mother paced. I didn't get the sense they were worried for my life, just for my future. My dad's way of reaching out was to tell me the story of the Prodigal Son. A parable of Jesus from Luke, the Prodigal Son is about a wastefully extravagant son who, after begging for his inheritance early, returns home broken and penniless. He asks his father to take him back as a servant so he can live, accepting also that this will end his relationship with his father. Instead, the father celebrates the son's return as a return from the dead.

I wasn't exactly welcomed home that way. My dad didn't order the finest calf slayed or throw a party. But so much of the parable rang true. His words calmed me. He always had that effect on anyone he wanted to truly affect. Years ago, one of my sisters' boyfriends killed someone and then drove over to our house out of his mind. Once my father realized what was going on, he sat the guy down, and soon had the guy driving with him down to the police station.

I didn't feel like a loser anymore, but I didn't feel in control either. I still didn't have a winning mindset. I wasn't sure how I was going to beat this. I was completely clean. I never called the construction site, where I knew I could get a job that paid in coke. But I had no idea what my next move was. I did whatever I could do. I worked on my correspondence course. I helped out with the high school wrestling team. I got some local catalog and a commercial ad work through an agency in DC. I hung out with my brother Patrick, who had graduated Penn State and was now working in town. Now he was the one looking to protect his older brother. None of it made me happy or really helped me survive financially, mentally, or emotionally. I was ready to run again.

And then Kirsten called.

I hadn't heard from her since my lockup in Switzerland. I had never done more than kiss her hello on the cheek, yet she lingered in my memory the way countless others hadn't. She was cool, smart, gorgeous even without makeup, and taken, which made me feel more relaxed. Our time together always felt easy, even if too many of our conversations were about helping her deal with her boyfriend. No other woman gave me that feeling, period. Sure, I could have driven her into my arms by telling her that her Milan boyfriend was stealing money from her, or tried to shake her free from that airhead in Vegas. But it wasn't my place or time. Until now.

Kirsten told me she had broken up with her boyfriend. She felt lonely and lost, and the first person she thought about reaching out to was me. She needed to get out of the city. Without checking with my parents, I invited her down to Falls Church. I told her to take the train to DC, where I'd pick her up at Union Station. I had grown a reddish-brown beard for the first time in my life. I made sure to say that before we hung up in case she didn't recognize me.

When I saw her come out of the station, I knew she was the one. I just *knew*.

The rain had started, so I jumped out of my brother's old green pickup truck in my military green designer raincoat I kept from Japan and ran toward her with my umbrella. She smiled when she saw me, and we walked arm in arm to the car. She asked me what I'd been up to. I decided to tell her everything, but not now. She looked tired, so I didn't push the conversation. We didn't exchange much but small talk on the ride, while I played tour guide and drove by the US Capitol, the Washington Monument, the White House, and the Lincoln Memorial. She couldn't believe I had a beard. All I could think was, *She is here…she is here…she is next to me…she is here.*

My parents never flinched when I told them Kirsten was coming, though I wouldn't have blamed them if they had. Most relationships in my life had been temporary. I didn't expect them to last long, and I didn't want them or me judged and scrutinized by my parents, who were expert interrogators. I told Kirsten to be ready, but whether because of the late hour or because they knew she would be there in the morning or just because they could see me smiling, my parents resisted the urge to start right in on questions. I set Kirsten up in the guest room with no more than a peck on the cheek before heading back to the basement to crash.

The next morning, I woke up late and headed upstairs for some coffee. I figured Kirsten was still out, and I made her some for when she got up. She is Norwegian and loves her coffee. Mug in hand, I wandered to the kitchen window that overlooks our backyard and the creek beyond it. It was a beautiful spring day, and I smiled at the smell of the air. I looked out into the backyard, and I saw her. Kirsten and my father were talking and raking leaves—an endless job at our house. For all the metaphors and messages for what my life was or was becoming that I had missed before, I didn't miss this one: the woman I wanted to love, surrounded by spring's promise, removing the dead leaves of the past, and connecting with my dad.

My parents loved her. We stayed about a week, and our bond was obvious to everyone who met us. Out with my old wrestling buddy Floyd, he leaned over when she was not looking and whispered to me, *John, you should marry her.* I believed she was the one who would help me find the way forward. But that wasn't going to happen living with my parents in Falls Church. We had only one marketable skill, and neither of us wanted to go back to New York to model.

That's when Kirsten said she knew Maggie's, the top agency in Boston, where she had worked before, and we decided it was a great option. They said they were interested, asked us to send up our pictures, and called back that day to tell us to come on up as a package deal. I stuffed my meager possessions in "The Bag," the giant blue duffel bag made famous when I showed up with it at a campus gathering toting a full keg of beer. I loaded my stuff and her belongings into the cab. We kissed my parents goodbye and caught the Amtrak out of Union Station.

Around New York City, a thought crossed my mind. *Hey, how did you know where I was and how to find me?*

I expected the answer to be divine intervention as surely her presence was a sign from God.

LEGORUB, she said.

What?

LEG-ORUB. You told me in Vegas and then Milan that if I ever needed to find you and didn't know where you were, your parents' phone number spelled (SOF) LEG-ORUB.

Maybe Kirsten was a sign from above, but at that moment I realized I was the one who had always controlled my destiny. I felt the very thing I longed for: love and stability. I knew I would share everything with her. I was finally running toward something, not away, and better yet, I wasn't alone.

MODEL ENGAGEMENT

KIRSTEN AND I FOUND a little apartment to rent at the Navy Yard in the Charlestown neighborhood of Boston, a ferryboat ride across the harbor to downtown. We bought a futon mattress. We watched a tiny Sony Watchman TV with a little antenna we moved around and around to get a signal. It was summer; all the college students were gone, and the nights were long. Every morning we made coffee and took the boat across the bay. The sea air refreshed us and set us on our way to our daily castings and appointments. Every evening, I went for a run over the bridge into downtown Boston and then back to Kirsten. *This is what a relationship feels like, huh?*

I had cheated on every girlfriend before Kirsten. Women were a game to me. It was all about my physical satisfaction: *What am I going to get out of it?* When I got bored, I upped the challenge of my conquests. *Can I keep this girlfriend and go and see a different beautiful girl that's interested in me?* When that got dull, I took it one step further. One year, I had the cover model on one side of campus and a cheerleader on the other, and they showed up to the same party. I'd run from one room to the other and kept it going all night. Even if I did get caught, I knew I'd be forgiven, because I was John Hanrahan. I later ducked out without saying goodbye and went to see my off-campus girlfriend, the lacrosse player who appeared in Playboy.

I was better now. I had learned in the light of my near death—in the source of truth and love—the power and beauty of unselfish love. That was what I longed for. My relationship with Kirsten was an intimate one built on a friendship. But what did I know about that? My parents liked her. My family and friends liked her. I knew I loved her. I had no idea what I was doing. *How am I going to hold this relationship together when I can barely take care of myself?*

So much for that winning mindset.

On top of my self-doubt, Kirsten and I had realistic concerns. Summer modeling work was limited. Most of our appointments were "go sees," meaning we went to see clients for consideration for shoots later in the season, but we needed money now. We had to score some work within the first month to stay afloat, and the fact that we hadn't was the first real test of our relationship. Our lease was month to month, and we had only paid for the first. I didn't know how to roll with life's punches with Kirsten; I didn't know if she could take the stress, and my worst instincts to run filled my head. I thought about bailing. *Shit, everyone was right about me.*

Suppressing one instinct only brought a slightly less bad impulse to the surface: I wanted to get high. Not cocaine, but pot. I got a joint from a guy across the hall and was going to just zone out and watch the Watchman. I didn't think it was a violation of my promise to stay clean and reflect the light. I wasn't addicted to pot. Pot hadn't killed me.

Kirsten exploded when she saw the joint. *What are you doing? You can't do that!* Why? *If you do that, I can't stay with you.* As we argued, our voices echoed around the futon in our otherwise empty apartment. I told her why I wanted to smoke, but Kirsten didn't back down. She didn't sound stressed or panicked like I'd expected. She sounded furious and like she cared about me—about us. She believed we'd find a way to survive. I realized I had crossed a boundary. I was humbled. I relented and flushed the joint down the toilet.

When we calmed down, we hugged each other. Her embrace felt like a silent, loving prayer. We fell asleep on our futon holding hands, and I felt strength and love from her and in her. Okay, pot was out too.

We went for a walk along the bay, and when we came back the phone was ringing. It was my booker from the agency. I had a casting call for a lucrative catalog job: five days of work at $1,200 per day—enough to float us in Boston for months. Enough to keep us together, to validate her faith and give me hope. I took a train out to the studio the next day to meet the client, along with every other male model in the city of Boston—it was a cattle call. After I waited my turn and presented myself and my book to the client, I believed I wasn't going to get it. I could see my book stood out among all the other guys in this room and this town, but it was an annual catalog for a uniform company, and this client probably wouldn't appreciate my international book of work.

Then I did something unexpected. I called my parents from a pay-phone at the train stop. My mom answered. Mom was usually the stoic, but she could hear the distress in my voice. I had always disguised my fears and worries related to my drug addiction, so she'd never wonder if something was wrong. I wasn't hiding now. *What's wrong, honey?*

My voice choked as I told her about the job and how if this job didn't come through, I didn't know what Kirsten and I would do—how I would hold together everything that felt right. The situation was different, but her solution was not: she told me she felt my pain and to pray, do the rosary, and that she and my father would pray for me too. This was the first time she'd told me that since I saw their prayers as pillars during my near-death experience. So I did it. I hung up the phone and sat alongside the railroad tracks and did a series of meditative prayers for fifteen minutes. I focused on the mysteries of life I had learned as a kid in Catholic school. I had no rosary beads, so I used my fingers to track the connected decades of prayers. I prayed toward the light that had given me this second chance. It comforted me until the train arrived. I jumped on with a sense of peace and acceptance of whatever God's plan was for me.

As I entered our apartment, the agency called. *The client loved you, you got the job.* I immediately took Kirsten out to a nice dinner. We called my mom and dad after dinner to let them know our prayers were answered.

I showed up on the studio set all week looking and feeling my best. I donned uniforms for every job sector you could imagine: security guard, chef, janitor, doctor…I even hung out between shots and genuinely got to know the client and his passion for long-distance biking. We talked about his family, and as I listened to him, I thanked God that my prayers somehow reached this soul, who choose me for this job and saved my relationship. A few weeks later, we escaped to Kirsten's mom's place in the Adirondacks—a beautiful, isolated hideaway called Camp Cobblestone that you could only get to by boat. It was an amazing place, with castle turret boat houses and several hundred-year-old cobblestone cabins and buildings along the exclusive lake.

Soon after we returned to the city, we were both making money. But it didn't feel real for some reason. I still didn't feel settled. Boston was not going to be home. I was worried that if I got too restless, I would fall into drugs again. I needed to keep moving, but I wanted Kirsten by my side. She listened as I revealed my twenty-something wanderlust. One night, I told her about what it was like working in Tokyo, how I had an agent in Japan, about Handa and our adventures and the money to be made there. I also told her cocaine couldn't find me there.

Kirsten had worked all the major markets of Europe but had never been to Asia.

Do you want to come with me to Japan?

No.

I pleaded my case. Boston was lovely, but we both knew it wasn't our final destination. We could go to Japan and have a beautiful apartment, and they'd pay for everything and advance us some money. She looked around at our futon and Watchman and coffee maker. It was near the end of the month. Rent was due. The fact that we'd have a fully furnished apartment in Tokyo was very appealing, she admitted—and she loved sushi. She finally relented.

I called Gloria Askew, and she was thrilled to bring us over as a couple. She quickly made arrangements to fly us to Tokyo and have an apartment ready for us, as well as work set up for the moment we arrived. I felt like a kid going back to Disneyland, and simultaneously like an adult looking forward to sharing a part of his past with someone he loved.

◆◆◆

WE ARRIVED AT GLORIA's office after the twenty-hour flight, and the Japanese booker proceeded to chase Kirsten around the office, wanting to *measure, measure, measure,* while I waited for our cash advance. I knew all the bookers, and I laughed the entire time. This was going to be great. Our private apartment was in the same fancy diplomat neighborhood as my two previous trips, and Handa was coming to pick us up in his signature red Ferrari for a double date with his girlfriend. Handa was still hooked up, with a beautiful house in the Azabu section of Tokyo. He also drummed in a rock band. Kirsten liked him immediately. She got that he had his own style and way of doing things, which was why clients let him do the storyboards any way he wanted.

The feeling was mutual. When Kirsten wasn't looking, Handa leaned over to me. *John, you should marry her...and you should wear a suit.*

The work started coming and I felt like a king again, only this time I had a queen. Instead of partying every night, Kirsten and I explored sushi restaurants. My cousin lived in Tokyo now and worked as an executive with Goodyear, and we spent Thanksgiving at his mansion in the outskirts of the city. In a bit of poetic synergy, Handa and his girlfriend took us to Tokyo Disneyland.

Not that everything was romance and Disney. Kirsten didn't get the kind of work she was used to in New York and Europe. She was getting tired of being booked for hair salon magazines instead of jobs like Ralph Lauren. Then came a painful reminder of Stefan and a sign of how things had changed in Japan: our friend Tristan, the son of British actor Alan Bates, died. He had been in good spirits when we saw him the day before. He had booked some modeling work in Southeast Asia and had gone for inoculations against malaria, cholera, and other tropical diseases in advance of the trip. That evening, he and his twin brother Ben met a bunch of people at a bar, and word got round that drugs, including heroin, were available. Tristan slipped away while Ben returned to his apartment. The next morning, Tristan's roommate rang Ben that Tristan never made it home the night before, which was very unusual for him. *Was he there?* Ben called us, and we said we hadn't seen him. We told ourselves that Tris was probably with a new girlfriend. By Sunday morning, there was still no word. Something was definitely wrong.

The Tokyo police informed Ben later that day that Tristan's body had been found in the public lavatory of a park in our neighborhood. The official word put out by Askew was that he died from an asthma attack, but none of us believed that. It was a stark reminder that my addiction might be suppressed, but it would never be gone. I thanked God for Kirsten's presence and resolved I would never let go of her. Handa's New Year's Eve party was coming up, and I decided that's when I would propose. I didn't have a ring, but I knew what I wanted to do.

Handa had told me about a Buddhist New Year's Eve tradition in which you make a vow or promise and then eat a piece of turnip, which is supposed to represent a part of your ancestors. You take them in with the vow, making it sacred. I had no idea if it was real, but it sounded powerful, and I used that moment to make my vow to Kirsten to be faithful for the rest of my life. As we stood alone by a quiet window, I explained the ritual. I then took out the turnip and said I wanted my vow to be devoting my life to her, and would she marry me? I ate the turnip and looked at her. Kirsten's eyes watered.

And then she sneezed. She had the flu and had only come because Handa had talked so much about the party and how much it meant to him. Then she said yes.

Kirsten looked at me and finally said, *Where's the ring?* Okay, her eyes behind the flu said that, but I sensed her confusion. Everyone got an engagement ring at the proposal. To bust my chops, when she called her mom, she said, *I think I'm engaged.* But I told her I had a plan. The next week, I had a job in Hokkaido, a stunning island in northern Japan. I stopped at the jeweler and bought a handmade sterling silver seashell ring. I raced back to Kirsten on the bullet train.

With our engagement now official, we started to think about what was next. We were three months into our Japan stay, but it felt even less real than Boston to both of us. We were living well but just playing house. And Tokyo was expensive. There was no way to live there if and when the modeling jobs dried up. By the end of January, we were ready to go.

We decided to face our demons in the only place we both felt we could survive: New York City.

◆◆◆

WE CAME HOME TO New York determined to find our way.

Since we needed a place to crash, our friend Augusto welcomed us for a couple of months in the spare room of his Upper West Side apartment. Augusto was an artist who survived by creating full-page illustrated ads for Bloomingdale's. He was later a sad victim of the plague of AIDS that took so many people we loved. Ravaged by the disease, Augusto took his life rather than decline further, ultimately slitting his wrists in a warm bubble bath. But in the days we stayed with him, Augusto was as boisterous and generous as ever. He was the kind of guy who made you laugh even when he told stories of how he was molested in a baseball dugout as a young kid in Venezuela. He and Kirsten got along like brother and sister. While we crashed with him, he helped me complete my Spanish course at Penn State, leaving just the math course to finish my degree.

Kirsten and I felt everything would be okay soon enough. We just needed to find our way. I was not going to go back to work with Ford (even if they would have me), but I had a meeting set up with another agency while I tried to figure out my future beyond modeling. Kirsten was looking for work too.

Then I relapsed. Not binges, and I never bought it myself, but cocaine filled the void a few times when a friend would hand me their stash and say, *Have a bump, Johnny*. I had to stay away from those friends, but to do that, I needed to figure out what was next. I never hid it from Kirsten. *Relapse is part of recovery. Relapse is part of recovery.* I said those words over and over. I was not clean, and it made me feel dirty. Yet she continued to believe in me. I felt unworthy. What if I brought our house down before it was even built?

When would this end? What did it mean?

I know we are all fallible. I know life is messy. I know we all succumb to temptation even in the best of times. But that did not help me then. It was like seeing an old friend who I knew I shouldn't hang out with—who wasn't good for me—but who I still longed to have fun with. We all have people like that in our lives. Mine was cocaine. But with Kirsten, I never completely lost control. I saw the lights all around her, and they guided me. I was holding on. I even wrote notes to myself in appreciation for her and the life and friendship around me. *We fuss and we fight when things get so tight. Hold on to your might and look for what's bright. Take pride in your plight—don't give up on the fight. A friend brightens things dim, hears all your sins, argues like kin, and backwardly bends.*

The street was dark and deserted as we walked home late one night except for a guy in a black jacket who appeared to be homeless. We got close to him and he asked for some help, I reached in my pocket to see if I had some loose change and he pulled a knife on us. *Give me your money, I'm not asking* is all he said, as he moved his right fist away from his jacket clutching a stubby, sharp shank toward my torso. I had no fear of so-called death, even though it was dark the lights were around me. I told Kirsten to run while I stayed, and then…I became my father. I calmly told the guy I didn't have any money and to put his knife away. No anger, no hate in my words. I understood my father in a new way in that moment. How he could look past any situation to slow things down and make anyone calm without fear.

That night, it didn't last. The guy came forward, and reached to grab my collar with his other hand, I grabbed his knife-hand wrist and banged him with my other forearm against the brick wall, just enough to knock his head and his knife to the ground. I got into ready position in case he charged again. But he left his shank and sprinted away in the opposite direction of Kirsten. I didn't want to celebrate, I was just glad my days of clouded judgement with drugs in my pocket were over. All I wanted to do was get a place with Kirsten and start making a home for real.

Later that week, Kirsten and I got our own apartment on East Forty-Fifth Street between Second and Third avenues. We packed up our "luggage" at Augusto's—a few Hefty bags and The Bag— and grabbed a cab downtown. We bought a futon and lay on it and wondered aloud what to do next. A couple of weekends later, Kirsten was looking at the want ads in the *Sunday New York Times* and tore out a listing. She handed it to me. *This is perfect for you.*

It said WANTED: PERSONAL TRAINER.

STAR POWER

ROD STEWART HAD JUST slammed into a wall.

I saw it coming. He had been plodding along on the treadmill at the Peninsula New York Hotel spa next to his supermodel wife Rachel Hunter, who ran effortlessly. Rod had pushed up the pace to try and match her speed. Sure enough, within a minute, his feet couldn't keep up, and he shot off the back, ass and elbows hitting the drywall behind him. He dropped to the floor with a thud. I had been his trainer on this visit. I moved to him discreetly to avoid any unwanted attention and helped him off the floor. I could tell he was hurt but refused to admit it. Ever the showman, he just switched to the Stairmaster and worked through the pain to prove he was okay.

Every picture tells a story, don't it?

It started a year before, with that job listing Kirsten found in the *Times*. 21st Century Health Club, just a few blocks north of our apartment, needed a personal trainer. I may not have been certified, but I knew training, the equipment, and how to teach. I called on Monday and explained my background as an All-American athlete. They asked me to come in, and I spoke to the manager about my wrestling career and mentoring underclassmen, the exercise science courses at Penn State, and the one-on-one strength training program I had done under Dan Riley, who was now a top strength coach in the NFL. I told the manager his club used the same line of Nautilus machines that Riley used to push me through high-intensity workouts. I got the job and started the next day.

It started a little scary with my first client, a Russian businessman who spoke little English. He managed to communicate to me that he wanted to be pushed very hard and refused to take no for an answer. I eventually accommodated him, though I knew he couldn't tell that I was still working him out only within reason. Then one day, as he completed his last rep on the chest press, he stood up, his face turned a dull shade of blue, and I caught his body as he fainted. I laid him out on the floor and yelled to another trainer to call 911. The businessman opened his eyes and sat up and smiled. He apologized and tried to explain. Finally I understood he was telling me he was lightheaded from not eating. He booked me for regular sessions over the next month.

I quickly stood out as the best trainer in the facility, not because of my looks or background but for my growing ability to put others first. I had empathy *and* the ability to motivate people and apply the appropriate level of stress for my clients to progress and get results. I got the empathy part from my mom. It laid a foundation for putting myself in other people's shoes as a trainer. I wouldn't be so quick to judge somebody for their physical limitations. I know I brought that to the table once I became a fitness and wellness professional. At 21st Century, I wasn't making $125 an hour like I did as a model, but it was steady work, and I enjoyed it. I would leave our studio apartment at 4:30 a.m. no matter the weather or temperature and bike up to the club to train my 5:00 a.m. private clients.

The motivation part I honed at Penn State with Dan Riley. He didn't yell, he just infused you with positive motivation. In turn, you worked your ass off for him, because he made you believe he was right there with you. I hated the weight room before I met Dan Riley. *This is the way you push and you move somebody and you help that person to bring out his or her best. This is how you regenerate, rejuvenate, and become stronger and able to handle more stress.* I loved redirecting the drive with my clients. I had to be their champion, channeling my energy to motivate others to reach their goals.

What I didn't love was the vibe of 21st Century. I sensed something was off for months, and not just because there was a muscle-head element—a number of clients who clearly used steroids hung out in the free weight area. Sure enough, my instinct was right. I biked up one Saturday morning, which I only did for certain clients, and the doors were locked and a sign said CLOSED. A crowd milled around outside. A few of them knew me and asked what was going on, but I had no idea. That same week, they had done a new membership drive with massive discounts for cash payments up front. Money had rolled in, and at the end of the week, they just locked up and left? Someone called the police. Someone called the news too, and soon a TV van pulled up from Channel 11 and started doing interviews. Arnold Diaz ended up doing one of his famous "Shame on You" pieces on the club's sleazy owners, who, among other things, had been taking cash for memberships and blowing it all on cocaine.

I gave thanks for two things when I heard that. First, that I had been oblivious to the coke that was right under my nose, or at least above my head, in the front offices. I had left that life almost completely behind. I didn't even care if I ever saw the dirty money I was owed for my last paycheck.

Second, that I had been moonlighting at an exclusive new club atop the Peninsula New York Hotel before it opened to the public. A guy who used to work at 21st Century had been the head trainer at the club since it opened for hotel guests, and he had recruited me weeks earlier. He knew my skill level and also my discretion; I had already taken on a few private clients and worked them out in their Manhattan homes. He invited me to check out the spa. I had never seen—or smelled—anything like it. Top-flight equipment mingled with the smell of fresh-cut flowers. Bright sunlight streamed through a wall of sparkling glass that overlooked Fifth Avenue. There was a crystal blue pool, bubbling hot tub, and relaxing terrace.

I met the GM, and we hit it off. After that, I was in for the hours they could use me. Then, just before the grand opening but after 21st Century closed, the Peninsula fired the guy who brought me in and made me the head trainer of what soon became the hot new exclusive club in the City.

Which is how I ended up helping Rod Stewart off the floor.

By that time, however, I already had a stable of devoted clients. Melanie Griffith, Jeffrey Koons, and Phil Collins sought me out when they were in town. I trained executives from companies like Chanel. Mercedes Ruehl worked out with me religiously in the years before she won the Academy Award for *The Fisher King*. She came in looking like a star and somehow left looking even better despite the workout I put her though. She was also one of the funniest clients I ever had. When I put her though a passive stretching routine, which she hated, I pressed her knees to her chest, and she'd say, *Whoa, be careful, you may unlock years of therapy with that move.*

Clients valued my discretion, and not just for my ability to pick them up without attracting attention after they wiped out trying to impress their hot supermodel wives. People would talk about everything they shouldn't when they worked out. One of my clients, a judge who had a high-profile case that was on the cover of the tabloids, confided in me that he believed the defendant was guilty as soon as he walked in the courtroom. The club valued my discretion, too. When an older gentleman complained that a younger man was masturbating in the steam room, I was the one chosen to confront the guy, revoke his membership, and walk him out after he got dressed. For some reason, the GM was so nervous about how to handle it that she gave him a gift-wrapped robe as I escorted him through the lobby. I was more concerned about what he did in our robes than with giving him one.

One day, I was leaving through the employees' elevator in the bowels of the hotel and came face-to-face with former president Richard Nixon, who had just done an interview for *60 Minutes* in one of the hotel's suites. He seemed relaxed, so much more alive than the way I remembered him looking when he resigned from office. He greeted me with a handshake, said hello, and told me I looked like a healthy young man.

He was right. I was—or at least getting there. Life was a dream during my time at the Peninsula, only it wasn't a fantasy like Japan. I was building a reputation and a career. Clients loved me and gave me generous tips and gifts for Kirsten. I trained a writer for the *Times* who wrote about our session.

I even felt good enough to return to my greatest love before I met Kirsten: wrestling. I didn't do it for me, though. I did it for her. Kirsten didn't know me as a wrestler or anything about wrestling. It had been five years since I stepped away from the 1984 Olympic Trials and let my New York Athletic Club team down. I decided to face my past and that shame; I entered the Club's international tournament at my current weight, 180.5 pounds. I wanted to show Kirsten the sport that had been such a big part of my life. I wanted to share that story with her. I wanted to write it for someone else—with someone else.

◆◆◆

AT THE WEIGH-IN THAT morning, I saw familiar faces from my previous life, including Sonny Greenhalgh, the president of the club who had blamed me for the club losing its national title. *Hanrahan? What the heck are you doing here? Are you going to wrestle? Oh boy, this oughta be good.*

Sonny thought I would crap out in the first round, and I did move cautiously through that initial bout against a Lehigh University kid. My knee joint felt vulnerable, but I steadied my approach and scored when I needed to. My aunt was in from Sag Harbor and sitting with

Kirsten. I heard their cheers as my arm was raised. That sound filled me up as I heard it again and again through the tournament. I ended up beating everyone in my weight class. At the awards ceremony, my old club coach, Iranian world champ Hamid Kermanshah handed me the champions' plaque. Sonny also shook my hand and handed me the Outstanding Wrestler award.

Wrestling wasn't about my ego anymore. It wasn't about making amends to Sonny or training for a world championship or the Olympics. I didn't care what anyone in the crowd thought, or even if they remembered who I was and that I had previously walked away. I wasn't addicted to their opinions. I wasn't trying to attract my sexual conquest for the night. I cared about only one person: Kirsten. Sure, I got to enjoy a taste of my old addiction, one that I never needed to hide from anyone. I got to see how far away I was from my Olympic training days. Could I go back? Could I still beat these young guys? Maybe I could. But I wasn't ready to come back to who I was. I was too busy becoming someone else.

I retired again.

I would not compete on the mat again for another eight years. But being on the mat felt great, and when a different kind of opportunity came along shortly after the tournament, I jumped at it. Jim Hill, a Fordham University math professor who knew me from the New York Athletic Club, asked me to coach the Fordham team that competed in the Metro Wrestling League. I accepted.

It was cool going up to the Bronx, where my dad was born and raised. This time felt much better than the last memory I had up there. When I was twelve, we'd visited my grandmother in her second-floor walkup apartment, and her German shepherd, Trinka, attacked me. The dog shredded my upper thigh, just missing my testicles. The whole episode ended with me being rushed to the hospital and a nurse clearing the way by screaming, *This boy's been bit in the groin!* My time with the young men at Fordham—and one girl who trained with us as part of the team, because a wrestler is a wrestler is a wrestler—was far safer and bite-free, and I loved my position with them. The job even paid me a huge dividend: Jim privately tutored me for my math correspondence course, and I completed my Penn State degree.

I was the last of the six kids in my family to earn a college degree, but I was the first and only one to do it completely on my own. I had almost paid with my life, but I had paid my own way.

I found myself wanting more out of life than I ever had before. I wanted to share with others what I learned the day I died, but knew the words I would use to describe what I was shown would always fall short and only frustrate me. I knew training celebrities and businessmen was not going to make that past go away, but my devotion to wellness was a penance for how I polluted myself. Still, I felt I was being dishonest. In my mind, I had to become somebody else to the people I trained—the somebody others wanted me to be. I wasn't an addict. I wasn't a model. I wasn't a wrestler who walked away from the sport he loved. I wasn't a guy who talked about his near-death experience and the light he had seen and still saw around us. I hid all that as a trainer because I believed no one wanted to be with that person, especially the addict. A part of me wanted to share all that, but the only way to survive was to go forward showing up as a new person. They teach you in recovery to "act as if." But I carried that baggage inside every day as I evolved as a trainer, never thinking hiding it would come at a cost.

There was only one part of my life that was one hundred percent true, and one thing left to do before I could complete my evolution with her and start a family.

It was 1990. Too much time had gone by since I had proposed to Kirsten in Japan. We set a date for our wedding in October in Sag Harbor.

GOT MARRIED TODAY

Bruce Weber, who introduced me to Kirsten on our *Vogue* shoot, came with his partner Nan and photographed us as his gift. It was a very special day as we gathered with family and friends, coaches, wrestlers, PT clients, and fashionistas in beautiful Sag Harbor. *Got married today*—those are the first words of the note I gave Kirsten that evening:

Got married today,
A most beautiful day,
Took the vows in the church
and felt a new birth
I now share my life
with an all-loving wife.
Got married today
what more can I say
God brought me a girl
beyond all of the world
I don't mean to boast
but I must make a toast
To Kirsten my bride
who fills me with pride.
Got married today

to please her I pray.
I now wear a ring
And the joy that love brings

Kirsten was pregnant soon after we were married, and we thought a lot about whether we wanted to raise a child in New York City, how expensive it was, and how far it was from our families. The company that ran the Peninsula spa had a club just outside of Washington, DC, close to my family in Falls Church. I told them what was going on, and they offered me a management position in DC—not great money, but enough.

Connor was born in DC, and everything was right in that moment. He was beautiful, and not just because he had two former international models for parents. He had a beautiful soul. Lights danced around him and filled me like nothing I had ever known short of my near-death experience. I had relapsed since I met Kirsten, but with Connor's light lifting me, I felt ever closer to the Creator, as now I was a cocreator of the life in front of us. I vowed never ever to betray the light and never to touch cocaine again—a promise I keep to this day.

The promise I could not keep was to be happy working in DC. It had its moments. I trained a White House executive who brought me a personal letter from President George H. W. Bush congratulating Kirsten and me on the birth of our son. I also spent time working out at the Washington Redskins' training facility with my exercise science mentor, Dan Riley, who was now the strength coach for the team. I completed advanced certifications as a strength and conditioning specialist with the NSCA and the NSPA and was a featured presenter at the NSCA national conference in DC. But still, after six months, I was bored. We weren't into the political game, and without politics DC had no pizzazz, no stars and no excitement. There was no real wellness movement. The president had just named Arnold, a former roided-up bodybuilder, as our nation's Fitness Czar. So much for promoting a culture of drug-free virtues to our youth. There was no devotion or real appreciation for the no-shortcuts training programs I was directing. I was ready to move on but held off telling Kirsten as long as I could. When I finally did, she revealed that she missed our life in New York City too. I started making calls and tracked down the former fitness director from the Peninsula. I had given him one of my private clients, who had since set him up with a company that managed health clubs all around the city. He said he had the perfect job and owed it all to me. He also had a perfect job for me, as general manager of my own club. I jumped on it. It was at the base of a luxury high-rise on the Upper East Side and paid enough to afford a doorman-staffed apartment nearby. Plus we could bring Connor to the club pool.

We moved into a beautiful building a block away from the club, and I started work immediately. Eventually I was given a second club to manage at the same time. I refused all but the most exclusive personal training opportunities and learned to run the business operations, hiring and firing, managing staff, and implementing systems. We lived the quiet, stable life we wanted, but in New York City, which suited us just fine. The best part of those days was that I reconnected with pieces of my fashion past, including training the head of the Ford Agency. He was the guy featured in *USA Today* for helping another model/actor recover from his addiction—the article my dad had sent me when I was in the throes of my own addiction. We talked about those days and how he could tell I was "hitting it hard." He had always hoped I would come to him and was happy to see me completely recovered.

I also began training Bruce Weber and his partner Nan Bush in Bruce's downtown loft, which I hadn't visited since I asked him to lend me money. I paid him back, telling him the first session was on me, and he laughed and acted like I never owed him anything. He then hired me to train the Abercrombie models in South Beach before a shoot. Like the Versace shoot years ago, when he had started the morning with the torture of an aerobics instructor, he still liked to put the models through a workout. Back then, I came in wasted to the Versace shoot. I was an agent of addiction, only interested in my obsession to get high. Now I was *his* agent of fitness, and it felt fantastic.

I think I could have lived that quiet life for the rest of my days if one of the club members hadn't told me about a trainer named Pat, who was opening an amazing new facility and looking for someone he could trust to work closely with him. She thought I'd be perfect for the role because I knew how to run a club and was an elite trainer.

Pat turned out to be Pat Manocchia, an exercise scientist I truly respected. He was more than just a trainer to stars like Madonna. Pat had the hookup with names that appeared everywhere from Page Six to the *Wall Street Journal*. He wanted to be known as more than a celebrity trainer and create more than just another swank and stunning health club. He liked what he heard on the phone—my technical training knowledge and ability, but also my attitude and my experience with both high-end celebrity clients and management—and wanted to meet. He told me to get ready: his plan was unlike anything anyone had ever seen. I was intrigued. Then he told me the name: *La Palestra*, Greek for "The Place for Wrestling."

When do you want to meet?

LA PALESTRA

PAT MANOCCHIA DESCRIBED HIS vision as a cutting-edge fusion of medical, health, and personal fitness services. It was preventative medicine taken to an entirely new individualized level at La Palestra, which would be more like a center for health than a traditional health club. Everything—from the trainers, the medical professionals, and the clients to the equipment and the unique space—would work together to achieve his vision. We had partnered with an internist, psychiatrist, physical therapist, registered dietitian, and nutritionist and bartered for their services in return for training. With this team, our club would function like a fitness and wellness university for members, who would get biannual assessments and workups. They'd then receive their semester objectives and take ownership of their health, from what they ate to the big goals they wanted to achieve. For all this, members would pay dearly—thousands more than any other club. But in return, memberships would be limited to those who could afford the fee *and* handle what La Palestra offered without needing to be coddled. Fewer clients, more individual attention? The model was unique at the time. The fitness club business was all about selling as many memberships as possible and packing people in. But even Pat's marketing would be low-key and completely word-of-mouth—not even a sign on the door. Just a doorbell and a camera, and if the receptionist recognized you, she buzzed you in.

Pat took me on a tour of the construction site: the old Grand Ballroom of the Hotel Des Artistes on Central Park West across from Tavern on the Green—the space that hosted the first Miss America pageant. It was a magnificent combination of scarred ruins, with old pillars and broken wall motifs fused with modern stainless-steel elements. Upstairs was a members' café/lounge, private changing and shower rooms, and an educational library. Downstairs was a wall of treatment rooms separated from the main room. On one side was a high-tech facility with cardio and modern Cybex weight machines, and on the other, an old-school gym with free weights, climbing ropes, a fencing area, and…the wrestling mats.

I shook hands with Pat on the spot and went to work executing his plan as vice president. I took everything I had learned up to that point, everything Pat wanted, and researched more to bring his vision to life. I poured all of it into binders of procedures and programs for Pat's review, and we refined, defined, and branded them. And when we opened our doors, Pat's connections and reputation had members lining up. Then *Vanity Fair* did a piece on Pat and the club, hailing our facility as a "shrine to fitness," and we were deluged with requests for membership. But we warned everyone—regardless of their celebrity or wealth—not to expect any special treatment. Everyone had to commit to the plan. La Palestra wasn't about being seen but being completely present. It was about seeing yourself in entirely new ways and pushing yourself. That's what we wanted people to want from us: no matter how wealthy or how famous, you were going to have objectives and put the work in to achieve them. Everyone agreed, but not everyone listened.

When I talk to people today about what we started at La Palestra, I get *of course* a lot, but nobody was doing what we did in 1990. We were providing individualized nutrition and psycho-wellness counseling before it was a thing. Diverse circuit-style training twenty years before CrossFit. Sport-specific program training as a structured journey toward achieving real goals and conquering actual events. Wellness linked to more than just working out but actual preventive medicine. We didn't train people just to be healthy; we taught people to own their health and much more. We wanted them to achieve in measurable and scalable ways, and we provided the expertise and motivation for them to get there. We made sure the staff, from the medical professionals to the cleaning people, were all aligned with this goal and had great chemistry. Everything and everyone had to work together to serve the clients' health and empower and motivate them. No pampering or stargazing allowed. Those who engaged—staff and client—thrived. Those who faltered failed.

Rosie O'Donnell was one of the many A-listers who was there at the beginning. Madonna referred Rosie to us. She had a new daytime talk show, and she wanted help with her fitness as her show started to get on track. Rosie dreaded seeing me and hated exercising but was a good sport, and I managed to get her through her workouts. She even talked about our relationship on her show: *My friend Madonna marries her trainer, and I tell John, who's my trainer, go away, go away. Anyways, he puts up with me.* We put up with Rosie, but she could not put up with our work-out conditions for long, and eventually she stopped showing up.

It didn't help her that Howard Stern was there at the start, too. Rosie was having a public feud with Howard and hated seeing him in the same room. But Howard was all in with Pat. Instead of going to the gleaming new Reebok Club that opened in his apartment building, he would come to La Palestra every day after his morning radio show. On the days we were wrestling, he'd stand mat side and say, *Look at you guys. You guys are like Neanderthals. You guys are animals.* I told him we had to get him on the mat. *No fucking way. You guys are freaking beasts. I think you guys are brain damaged.* Then he'd go attack the stationary bike, his long curly hair tied back in a bandana. He really was the nicest and most genuine guy, though that wasn't the image he projected on the show. New people would ask me, *Who's the guy who thinks he's Howard Stern?* But it was who he was. He was all in for his training and never stopped coming.

John F. Kennedy, Jr. and I bonded over the fact that when he was born, I was down the hallway in the same DC hospital, an eight-month-old baby being treated for pneumonia. He loved to vary his training and took whatever I threw at him. Walking lunges while carrying a weighted Olympic bar with plates across his neck? A mix of heavy-duty circuit modalities? He loved it all. One day he was finishing some ab work on the wrestling mat, and my son Connor came running into the gym and jumped right on his gut, knocking the wind out of him. John just laughed like it was part of my workout plan. Sure, he sometimes felt like an accident waiting to happen— once as he was leaving on roller blades, I reminded him about his bike. I'll never forget him pedaling off to Central Park on his bike with his roller blades still on his feet, but that's just who he was, fun-loving and fearless. He charmed everyone, and as *People's* "Sexiest Man Alive," the girls who freshened up the locker room never complained that he left every towel in the place on the floor between his locker and the shower.

I worked regularly with Natasha Richardson as her trainer, while her husband, Liam Neeson, liked to box and hit the heavy bag old-school style on his own. They gave Kirsten and me a baby jogger. I loved taking Betty Buckley for runs in Central Park. She was starring in *Sunset Boulevard* on Broadway, and everyone knew her from *Cats*. But I remembered her from TV's *Eight is Enough*. She left tickets for Kirsten and me to see her show and got mad when we didn't come backstage to her dressing room afterward. We didn't know that's what she wanted. Yet that's the kind of intimacy our clients felt with us. Nowhere was that connection deeper than with the billionaire philanthropist Howard Gilman and his company's executive president Natalie, who began as Howard's secretary. They would train every morning, and on Fridays Natalie would give out

$100 bills on behalf of Mr. Gilman to the entire staff. Pat had gotten Howard's health on the upswing after a series of heart surgeries, and Howard believed in Pat and his vision so deeply that he had funded our launch. Childless himself, Howard made the La Palestra family his family. He flew us on his private jet down to White Oak Plantation, his wildlife preserve in northern Florida, which his family had owned for generations. We'd dine in the main lodge and adjourn to the living room, where a wildlife expert brought a young cheetah over for us to pet. One time, Kirsten and I flew down with Connor joined by Mikhail Baryshnikov, his wife, and his little girl, who was Connor's age. Baryshnikov headlined the White Oak Dance Project, which Howard also funded. The kids loved the game room with the giant stuffed polar bear and the bowling alley, and Howard loved seeing them play. He was simply the most gracious host you could imagine, and as he worked to live a longer life, he inspired us to be better every day.

Word about La Palestra soon spread beyond New York City. Hollywood celebrities would come by when they were in town to work with us. Jerry Seinfeld became a regular. Julia Roberts liked to be treated like one of the guys. One morning she came in after a night out with Pat and his gang, during which she got drunk and danced on the bar in her bra at Coyote Ugly. She was all over the front pages of the tabloids. Yet she fought through the embarrassment and the hangover to finish her workout. She even asked me to teach her wrestling.

I wasn't on the town with them that night. Not that I wasn't invited, but after I finished work, I became husband to Kirsten, father to Connor, and expectant dad of our second son, Liam, who was on the way. In the evening, I'd take Connor in his stroller up to Park Avenue and Ninety-Sixth Street to watch the trains burst out of the tunnel toward Harlem. We'd station ourselves right above the tracks. When one train burst out of the tunnel so loudly it vibrated the sidewalk, Connor looked up at me. *What was that, Daddy?*

I told him it was a diesel train. As we headed back home, Connor looked up at me. *Daddy, I think we should name the new baby Diesel!* I sometimes think back and marvel: *Did he have an early premonition about Liam's unique, hard-driving personality?*

If I went out as an adult, it was usually with Kirsten alone, on a date. Tim Zagat was a client and he got us reservations at Rosa Mexicano for my birthday, which we'd never have been able to get on our own. We almost didn't go, as Kirsten started going into labor before we left the apartment. But we kept calm and decided to go— and got treated like royalty the moment we walked in the door, thanks to the power of the Zagat name. Rosa greeted us personally as we arrived and comforted Kirsten by telling us that she wouldn't be the first person to go into labor at the restaurant. We finished dinner and headed to Mount Sinai Hospital, where we welcomed Liam just after midnight. He got to have his own birthday, as mine had just ended.

In the hospital room *David Letterman* was on TV, and I listened as *Good Morning America* host Joan Lunden, who worked out with me regularly, talked with Dave about her "personal summit" and reaching the top of Mount Hood, a goal my training helped her achieve. We always pressed our clients to get away from the aesthetic goal of just looking better in the mirror and to find something—like a mountain climb or a marathon—to accomplish that they could be proud of. Too many trainers created fake activities and staged events to prop their clients up. At La Palestra, we compelled them to go for something bigger, something real. We'd then program their training to achieve that goal.

Joan had achieved that. Sandy Hill Pittman, wife of the media mogul Bob Pittman, was trying to go to an even bigger summit: Mount Everest. She had made it to the top of the six other great peaks and wanted to be only the third woman at the time to scale all seven. She prepared hard for this challenge, but the story of what happened on her climb became the subject of magazine features and even a movie: the worst human disaster in Everest history, with seasoned climbers never making it off the mountain. Sandy, who *Vanity Fair* called "Everest's Socialite Climber" in a scalding feature, unfairly bore the brunt of the blame, as if the disaster only happened because she was there. Nothing could have been further from the truth. I saw firsthand and helped administer the grueling training she put in to prepare for her quest. The whole sad story was a reminder that life is full of risks and many risks come with great costs.

That's when I started thinking: What had anything I'd done cost me? What had I done to achieve any goal in my time at La Palestra? My strength as a trainer had always been empathy and motivation. How had I applied that to myself?

Just before Kirsten became pregnant with Liam, I had been on a run and decided that pressing clients like Joan and not myself had made me a hypocrite. That I was thirty-five was just an excuse for not trying. We got people hooked on huge goals. I was training people to believe they could achieve them. They had the winning mindset that I had lost more than a decade ago. It had been eight years since I abandoned wrestling and eleven since I gave up my dreams of being an Olympic and World Champion in 1984. *What a hypocrite.*

That was it. I decided to return to wrestling and train immediately for the 1996 Olympic trials.

◆◆◆

OF COURSE, EVEN WITH my commitment to train for the Olympics, I still was a hypocrite. When I told my client, MTV founder Bob Pittman that I used to see his VJs going in the MTV studio on Fifty-Seventh Street from my apartment window, I left out that we called my place the Pleasure Dome. I had risen to the pinnacle of training, health, and wellness in New York City, and no one knew how deep a hole I'd had to climb out of to get there. I thought about this every day, but I had told my story to no one since I started my training career. I didn't know what people would think of me if I did, and

I didn't want their judgment of my wellness story, even if I was passing judgment on theirs.

Judge not, lest ye be judged? That was not part of my work gospel. While I had close relationships with Pat and so many of our clients, I didn't trust myself and feared what would happen if I came clean—even if I was clean now. Besides, my job was not to over-share. *How many trainers never realized they were fired because they talked too much?* I had honed this skill with the star power at the Peninsula, limiting my conversations to listening and learning about each individual, exploring what they wanted, and letting them relieve their stress. At La Palestra, I worked to find the right health prescription to move each client forward. At the conclusion of each training session, I provided those clients with my signature, ten-minute hands-on passive stretch routine, during which they would relax, let go, and focus only on their breathing. I infused each minute with both technical expertise and the light that I saw around them. I silently prayed for every individual I touched and sought to radiate love, truth, and goodness to comfort their souls.

There was always something special about my hands for me. My sister had touched my hands to relieve me of my night terrors as a child. Now they gave me that power in reverse: putting my hands on my clients, I could feel their energy as I opened them up and they opened up to me. I took it as the ultimate compliment that they would share their inner thoughts or things that were bothering them. I didn't have the answers, and they didn't expect me to. I just listened the way a therapist would. Then, as our relationships progressed, I learned to recognize when to infuse my own side of the conversation with opinions and appropriate personal stories.

But never *that* part of my story. *Why even start?* Telling it had never made me feel better, only worse. *This person can't comprehend what happened to me.* No one ever had. *I'm the fountain of health. Will they see me in a different light? Will they think I'm not capable anymore? Will they think I'm weak? Will they think I'm not everything that they were promised?* I made sure never to show up with bad breath or reeking of cologne so even the smallest things would never stand in the way of me inspiring them to achieve their goals. This was not a small thing that could be fixed with an Altoid. *Could I have helped someone, let alone myself, if I did share?* I didn't think that way anymore; that was not the performance I was giving on this stage or the message I was tasked with delivering.

I did try—once. Sandy Gallin, Hollywood mogul and legendary manager of Michael Jackson and so many others, hired me to train him in Central Park on his trips to NYC. I met him at his Fifth Avenue apartment, which he shared with his longtime friend and business partner Dolly Parton, and invariably waited thirty minutes while Sandy finished a call. Dolly would sometimes be there and pour me some coffee; she even let me see her without makeup. *Oh honey, nobody sees me without my makeup, but you're like family— come on in.* As soon as Sandy was off the phone, we'd buzz out the front door for a one-hour walk/run. Some days our walks diverted to the antique shops on Fifth Avenue, where the owner railed behind Sandy, who picked out beautiful rare pieces without asking their price and had the store call his assistant to have them shipped to Lowell, his butler, at the house in Los Angeles. Then, just like that, we were out the door and back on our walk. That was Sandy—a bon vivant if there ever was one.

As we walked, I could see that countless to-do lists and ideas jumped and fluttered in Sandy's head, wanting to come out. But I didn't push. I waited for him to open up to me. When he did, I was moved in a way I had not been with any other client. I expected to hear something about Michael Jackson or the other gossip that people wanted him to write a book about. Instead, he told me he had been sick and doctors had expected him to die. He promised God that if he lived he would give thanks to Him the rest of his days. Sandy was Jewish, and when he spoke, he pulled out his *tallit*, or prayer shawl, and *tefillin*, or scrolls, which he wrapped around his arm and head before he prayed. His prayers, like everything Sandy did, were uniquely his. He started with an Our Father in English followed by a mash-up of prayers in Hebrew. His words were him keeping his promise to God, thanking Him for allowing him to live, and cherishing the miracle of each new day. I would bow my head with him and pray for him and all souls, and then tell him I was there to remind him to get it done. He always, *always* finished each prayer by giving thanks for me and asking for blessings for *John Hanrahan, Kirsten, and their boys Connor and Liam.* Then we'd get moving.

As this became Sandy's and my shared pattern for our visits—prayer, then workout—I felt his prayers supporting all of us and wanted him to understand just how much that meant. I decided to tell him my story. He had let me in so deep, I would do the same for him. I felt safe to be vulnerable with him because he was vulnerable with me. You would never expect that side of Sandy Gallin unless you knew him, but I felt love and unselfishness from him.

So one day, after the prayers and bolting out of the apartment to the park, I saw the lights bouncing in the bright sky, and it felt right to share what I had been through for the first time in a decade. Sandy soaked it all in. He didn't respond at all as we walked. I didn't feel like he judged me. Sandy never railed against drugs; he worked with plenty of successful addicts and users. He himself was a celebrity fixture among the early cocaine-fueled Steve Rubell, Studio 54 crowd of the late seventies. We talked about the craziness. I knew what I said stayed with him, just as my clients knew what they said to me stayed with me.

Still, as I openly and honestly spoke about my addiction and dying from a drug overdose, the fact that he just listened started to make me self-conscious. I wasn't getting what I needed back. What that was, I did not know, but I needed something, and I was getting frustrated, the way I had the first time I tried to tell my story, only this time because someone wasn't disputing it. He wasn't doing *anything.* When I told him about crossing over, he didn't probe for details. When I told him about coming back, he didn't deny that it was possible. I found myself trailing off. I never really got to the end. I've learned there is no end in trying to describe to others what I was shown.

Ultimately, I did not regret telling Sandy my story, but I quickly pushed it back inside me and went back to maintaining the carefully crafted image of health I had taken to the highest levels at La Palestra. What they needed to know was that I was with them on their journeys. I was all in for my return to wrestling, and those Olympic trials were coming up. Wrestling would have to be my next step forward. I didn't need to share my story. Kirsten and the boys made me feel whole and had helped me put my cocaine addiction behind me for good.

This time, I wasn't looking for wrestling to fill the void cocaine left, but to give me the space to deal with what life threw at me, to further renew my soul and reflect the light I saw. Sure, I knew it would be painful to endure the intense physical training required, but I was ready to suffer and hoped the effort might exorcise the demons of my past. Kirsten didn't love that I was doing it—didn't love that it meant more of the burden of caring for our boys fell on her alone and that she would be without me more often—but she saw I needed it. *I wanted it.*

REBORN IN WRESTLING

WHILE I BELIEVED I could reclaim what I had lost and pursue my two longtime wrestling dreams, I had one problem: I couldn't do it alone. Making the commitment was one thing, but I had no one to work out with on the level I needed.

The solution came from the most unlikely of people: a makeup artist. She was working a shoot at La Palestra and told me a current world wrestling team member, Rico, was in New York City. Not only that, he was working as an actor/model at the Ford Agency.

Rico was the real deal. I saw him coming up the ranks as a junior national champion from Baltimore. He won an NCAA championship at the University of Iowa in 1987 and the USA senior freestyle championship in 1989. I called Ford and invited Rico to La Palestra. I told him my wrestling mats at the most exclusive club in the City were open for training. He came right away, and I liked him immediately, especially when he showed up with another world team member. The three of us began our training runs, lifting, and wrestling sessions.

The first week of training with them shocked my body. I could barely move. It was painful but that was what needed to happen. For the Olympic trials, I had to tear my thirty-six-year-old muscles down through shock and awe, and then build them back up to beyond the level they were when I was in my prime. I was twelve years removed from the way I should have prepared in '84. I was doing it right this time and exorcising the demons of my past in the process.

As if I needed to be reminded of how long ago that prime was, another wrestler and world cup champion came in with Rico one day, looked at me, and shouted: *John Hanrahan! I can't believe it! I used to watch you as a kid when you were at Penn State! You were like a god. Us kids would look at you and say, look at that guy's muscles. We wanted to be like you.* I would have liked to be like me then, too. This guy was talking about a version of me from close to twenty years ago. Twenty *years*. Seven years since I'd wrestled competitively.

Yet even if the old me could somehow travel through time and take my place, he would have found a familiar foe waiting for him on the mat: Dave Schultz. While I had abused my body with drugs and alcohol for more than a decade, Dave had maintained his. The only upside was, I hadn't really worn my joints out wrestling since I backed out from challenging Dave and Lee Kemp in 1984. Aside from entering the New York Athletic Club tournament in 1988 and coaching at Fordham for a few seasons, I had not put my body through anything this stressful in a long time, and I felt it getting stronger. Still, I knew I had a long way to go to even think about challenging Dave— or anyone else. After all, it wasn't like everyone just took a seat for ten years while Dave won everything. There was more than Dave in my way, especially three-time All-American Kenny Monday from Oklahoma State. Monday had broken the color barrier at the 1988 Summer Olympics and become the United States' first black gold medalist in the sport, inspiring an entirely new generation of diverse wrestlers. Just like when I was at my peak, my weight class was the most competitive in the country and the world. I knew I needed to do more. My mindset was about winning. I would not walk away.

In December 1995, eight months into my training in New York, I decided to join Dave Schultz and head down to Delaware to John DuPont's wrestling mecca, Foxcatcher Farm. Yes, the same

Foxcatcher they made a movie about. The place was run by the DuPont Chemical heir who took the life of my rival before I finished my quest to face him one last time.

I rented a car and drove down with Kirsten and the boys. The scene was surreal. On the one hand, it was the wrestling mecca I expected. DuPont was USA Wrestling's cash cow and he had created the top club team and training facility. Foxcatcher had everything you could want, and the guys who had deals with DuPont lived in their own houses on this big estate and got paid for being there. On the other hand, John Eleuthère du Pont was everything the movie made him out to be and more. About the only thing that was truly fiction was that Mark Schultz, Dave's brother, never lived on the estate at the same time. Mark had left Foxcatcher in 1988, before his brother even arrived and long before the murder happened.

I was grateful to have my family and a few people I knew well with me at Foxcatcher, including Rico and Greg Elinsky, a former Penn State wrestler who I helped recruit and then coached at Penn State my Grad-Assistant year. Kirsten hung out with Elinsky's wife, and she told Kirsten if John du Pont came down the hallway or into the room not to look at him. *Don't look the guy in the eye.* Kirsten never saw him, and du Pont never said much to me. He had the mannerisms of a paranoid addict; I had seen many. One of the guys told us he was a ticking time bomb. We heard how he threatened guys with guns. How he drove a car into a lake and bailed out to swim to shore, and then laughed while his passenger barely escaped. How he burned down the house of one light heavyweight he felt had crossed him. Threatened a wrestler by pointing a machine gun at him. How he'd had all the cardio machines at Foxcatcher removed because he called them "time machines." How he removed the color black from the farm, including the black athletes.

I resolved to watch my back and stay only as long as I needed to, which turned out to be about four days of high-level training with some great wrestlers. That boosted my confidence in advance of the

New York Athletic Club tournament in January. I ended up missing that tournament because of a MRSA forearm infection, but I went to the club anyway to watch, just like Coach had told me to do when I crapped out of the NCAAs nearly two decades before. I saw Dave, who was there to coach Team Foxcatcher, and I took him out that night to my friend's Christmas party. It was the last time I saw Dave Schultz alive.

Dave returned to Foxcatcher that day, and on January 26, 1996, du Pont shot him three times point blank outside his family's home on the estate. He died in his wife Nancy's arms as du Pont drove away. John du Pont holed himself up in his mansion until he was captured. He was tried, judged to be mentally ill but not insane, and sent to jail for murder.

Kirsten and I heard the news the day it happened. At first, the TV only read "Breaking News: Olympic Wrestler Murdered." We looked at each other and said, *Du Pont killed Dave. He killed Dave.* The next day, Diane Sawyer, who I'd trained but who had a problem showing up for her sessions, showed up early. In fact, she didn't even have a training scheduled. She knew I knew Dave and wanted my help getting the exclusive interview with his wife Nancy. I agreed to call and ask, and Nancy said yes. Diane filmed the interview on our La Palestra wrestling mats.

Dave's tragedy notwithstanding, the Olympic events went on as expected. I entered the East Region Trials and won four matches against guys much younger than me before losing 2–1 in the finals. It was a great showing for my La Palestra family—no one had expected me to make it more than a match or two as a just-out-of-seven-year-retirement thirty-six-year-old—and the close match I lost in the finals only reaffirmed the return of my winning mindset. I may have fallen short of my Olympic dream again, but I was back in wrestling and determined to push myself farther.

I relished everything about the opportunity to be back on the mat—even my new "cauliflower ear." Cauliflower ear is what happens when a wrestler takes repeated hits that cause hematomas to clot and block the flow of blood to the ear. The ear must then be drained of the fluid before it hardens in its blown-up state, sometimes to the size of a golf ball. The ear actually does look like a cauliflower floret. I loved my deformed fluid-filled ear even if Julia Roberts let me know she didn't. Besides, Julia, I'm taken—though Kirsten didn't like it much either. *Too bad—I'm a wrestler again.*

As a La Palestra trainer drained my ear for me, I watched as she took out the syringe and thought to myself, *The last time anyone stuck a syringe in me was the morning I died.* I said nothing. I had been given a second chance to compete in this sport without blow, and I was not going to blow it this time by giving up or distracting myself with tales of my past. I resolved to double my training efforts before competing at the US Open in Vegas.

While I wouldn't get my chance to wrestle Dave Schultz again, I did end up wrestling *for* him in Vegas, entering the event as a representative of the newly formed Dave Schultz Wrestling Club founded by his widow, Nancy. I hadn't been to Vegas since the *Vogue* shoot with Bruce Weber, where I met Kirsten for the first time. I had left Vegas after that trip on the way to the worst shape of my life. I returned in the best shape of my life—and I needed to be, because my first match was against the 1992 NCAA Champion, Ray Miller.

I had watched this guy win his title a few years earlier. He was tough, still in his prime, and too young to know who I was. This was the test I wanted. The boys were too young to come to Vegas, so Kirsten stayed behind with them. Rico was in my corner. I looked at him, and I knew I was ready. I pulled up the straps of my stars and stripes USA singlet.

The whistle blew, and I engaged, fighting for control and positioning, scrapping and clawing my way to a hard-fought two-point victory that ended with Ray on his knees, punching the mat in frustration. I knew that feeling of being humbled. It was a much better feeling dishing it out. He stood and shook my hand, and as my arm was raised, Rico gave me a nod and a smile. I won four more matches before losing to national champion Marcus Mollica when he got me in a high-flying body lock. Kenny Monday went on to win the tournament and represent our weight class in the 1996 Atlanta Olympics. But what stayed with me wasn't my losing or Monday winning. It was Ray Miller's face after he lost and looked up at me with eyes that said, *Who is this guy?* A wrestler, Ray. That's who I was. *A wrestler.*

Before leaving the arena, I made my way to the medical tent and got in line behind five other guys waiting to get our swollen ears drained. The nurse stuck the syringe in, drained it, and since I was finished wrestling, she clamped my ear with what looked like a metal money clip to hold it in a compressed state. The clip had to stay on for five days. I wore it and all the aches and pains and scratches on my face with pride. I was a wrestler again, one who deserved to be considered with the best in his country. With my performances in 1996, I had put myself in the position to wrestle at a high level again. I still aspired to reach a world championship podium wearing the USA singlet, but I also aspired to something more: stability.

Kirsten and I had once again decided we needed to give up New York City. La Palestra was everything I imagined, but making ends meet in Manhattan with two children, one in an expensive Upper East Side, Park Avenue preschool, made us consider other options. We just didn't want to make the same mistake we had the first time, leaving New York and finding ourselves bored.

We didn't.

LA LA LAND

Sandy Gallin was the one who encouraged me to come out to Los Angeles. While telling him my story hadn't had the impact I'd hoped for, we stayed close and worked out together every day he was in New York City. But if you know Sandy, that was not enough. He wanted me in LA and said he would commit to having me train him two hours a day, seven days a week *forever* (meaning every day he was in LA), which would be enough money to live on while I built my business with referrals and new clients.

First, Sandy invited me to come out to his West Hollywood mansion as his guest to try it out. When I arrived at his gated home off Doheny Drive, I was in awe. Impeccably manicured bushes, flowerbeds, and beautiful trees surrounded the slow-winding driveway. Sandy's housekeeper, Cora, a small Philippine woman who's a firecracker and not afraid to speak her mind, greeted me at the door and walked me through the latest home Sandy had renovated and decorated himself. Soon I knew he would throw a lavish party to show it off and then flip it to one of the guests or some Hollywood star—a habit that began when Frank Sinatra bought Sandy's home "as is" (furniture and all) after a party years ago. Lowell, Sandy's butler and chef, took over from Cora, and I got the full tour on the way to my guest room. As we walked, I noticed some of the lamps and artwork Sandy purchased during our New York City buying-spree workouts. Lowell showed me the gym and then took me to Sandy, who was on the phone, of course. We eventually got to praying and working out for an hour.

Sandy's pitch became more and more compelling in the days I stayed with him. Los Angeles certainly had more affordable places to live and opportunities to thrive. Liam and Connor would love the beaches and warm weather. Kirsten would have more space to breathe. I could try and make it on my own. Gerry Laybourne, the president of Nickelodeon, who I'd trained in NYC, introduced me to the owner of the gym she trained in. Howard Stern, Betty Buckley, Graydon Carter, Natasha Richardson, Michele Anthony, and others were all happy that they would now have me as their West Coast trainer. About the only person who said she hated the idea was Julia Roberts. She was working the treadmill and never broke stride as she said, *Don't go to LA. Why would you live in LA? I hate LA!* I tried to explain to Hollywood's highest-paid actress that it was in my family's best financial interest and that she had to trust me, this was the right move. *Okay, but I think you're making a big mistake.*

Of course, there was a chance we *were* making a mistake, but Kirsten was on board. This wasn't wanderlust. There wasn't a single thing we were running away from. We were making it in New York, but we wanted to make it in the future too. We were running to opportunity without fear of the boredom that affected us in DC. Sure, we'd be far from our families, but they would want to visit us in California, and we could always come home for holidays. Saying goodbye to Pat and our tight-knit La Palestra family was hard, but Pat understood what Julia didn't. Besides, he now had an LA trainer he trusted to send his clients to on their inevitable trips west.

And that was that. We loaded up our Toyota and piled in the car for our cross-country odyssey. We played *The Polar Express*, read by William Hurt, over and over again because it soothed the boys on the long drive. We ended up renting a small two-bedroom house with a huge backyard in El Segundo, a beach town nestled south of LAX. Our neighbor turned out to be a fellow Penn State alum and wrestling fan who also had two sons, and our families hit it off immediately. At Connor's birthday party, his entire first-grade class—thirty-five kids, plus the parents who stayed to welcome us to LA—filled the yard, along with a bouncy house, a clown with balloons, and Darth Vader. Even my TV and movie star client Mary McCormack came down from Hollywood. I don't think we could have fit that many people in our lobby in New York, let alone our apartment.

It took a little longer for me to get into the Hollywood scene. When Sandy went away on a private yacht for three weeks, we temporarily lost a lot of our income, but I never felt the need for drugs—never felt the need to run again. Kirsten and I had faith in each other and our choice, and when Sandy returned, his connections and word of mouth paid off. My client base began to snowball. We were all-in on Los Angeles, and I gave the performance everyone expected.

◆◆◆

MY LA DAYS ALWAYS involved Sandy, two hours a day seven days a week. Most days, we trained in his Hollywood home, but sometimes we'd grab mountain bikes and ride canyon trails with Barry Diller, who invited us to his place for Sandy and Barbra Streisand's birthday celebration. Sometimes our training sessions turned into house-buying expeditions. One day, he bought Flip Wilson's old house on the Malibu beach and rented the house next door. He had the house rebuilt so it looked like a country house in the Hamptons. Sandy's attention to detail was meticulous, and he had no tolerance for anything except exactly what he wanted. When the floors did not look naturally distressed like an old farmhouse floor, he was furious with the foreman. *Anyone can tell you made these marks with a sander!* Then Sandy got on his knees and mimicked going back and forth with a belt sander. When it became my job to do the gyms in the homes he designed, I never betrayed a single detail of his vision, lest I endure his wrath.

After I trained Sandy in the mornings, I'd train clients back in town, constantly networking and building up my client base. Our used Toyota stood out from all the gleaming new cars in the neighborhood, but soon I had connections the other LA trainers could only dream about, including Donald De Line—the president of Touchtone Pictures, which is owned by Disney—who personally set our family up at Disneyland. I told him about what we did at La Palestra, training people to achieve big goals like marathons. He was up for making that his thing, and every morning we ran down Sunset Boulevard or the beach as we built up his stamina. Then came the day, on our usual run together, that he just stopped and looked at me. Not because he was exhausted, but because he was anything but: he realized that he was going to accomplish his goal. His eyes watered as he spoke. *Hanny, you don't know how much this means to me. I used to get teased in high school because I was this pudgy kid who couldn't do anything, couldn't even run.*

My throat choked up. My voice cracked as I responded. *I'm proud of you and all the hard work and training you have done to reach this goal. Thank you for putting your trust in me along the way.* Hanny the redeemer—and still seeker of redemption—helping others find their strength. Another step into the light.

My work with Sandy and Donald led to more and more work: David Geffen, Tim Burton, Amy Pascal, Jane Berliner, Ron Meyer, Kevin Huvane, Bryan Lourd, Annabella Sciorra, Rick Rubin, Davis Guggenheim, Michele Anthony, Gerry Harrington…the list of names kept growing. On a typical day, I'd have Sandy, Donald, Kevin, David, and then any combination of other stars and moguls. Patricia Heaton, the star of *Everybody Loves Raymond*, bonded with me over the fact that her high school sweetheart was an Iowa wrestler whom I had competed against. Sandy Hill, now divorced from Bob Pittman, called me up and asked me to train her and her new fiancé

Tom Dittmer in Santa Barbara, which was a haul, but she insisted she would make it worth my while and even fly me on her plane. Beverly D'Angelo had me come to the Spanish-style mansion in the Hollywood Hills that she shared with her boyfriend, Al Pacino. He'd watch us talking and working out, and when I'd look over at him, he'd quickly duck behind a wall. He didn't like the intimacy of my signature hands-on stretch at the end of our workout. Beverly laughed and told me not to mind him, though I had to remind myself he wasn't really Scarface.

My New York clients would also seek me out when they came west. I would pick them up and take them to the private training gym I rented or else work them out around Los Angeles. Cyndi Lauper regaled me with stories about the spirit dancing she had been doing in the hotel, and I told her that would count for her cardio. Howard Stern would tell me to call him at the hotel under his fake name, and I'd pick him up in my little Toyota, with the passenger seat pushed all the way back and reclined to fit his long frame. One day, I took him for a run in the Beverly Hills neighborhood next to the gym. A tour bus coming down the road spotted us and turned around. Everyone leaned out the window screaming, *Howard! Howard!* Howard just looked at me and said, *Look at those freaking idiots.* In a nice piece of synergy, I also trained Mary McCormack, who played Howard's movie wife in *Private Parts*. He was divorcing his real wife at the time, which we avoided discussing.

None of my initial clients came from advertising; it was all word of mouth, like it had been at La Palestra. That is, until media attention pushed me over the top. *Allure* proclaimed me "The Best Personal Trainer in Los Angeles," and I made it back in *GQ* for the first time since the Rico Puhlmann shoot when they named me one of the "12 Guys You Should Know." Me. The guy you *should know for fitness.* Demand for my time only increased. I was working so nonstop that I hadn't had time to think about how I'd achieved my goal: for the first time in my life, I was my own boss. I was being paid the same $125 hourly rate, and more, that I commanded as a top model, without being beholden to anyone but my clients and myself. I loved it. And I wanted more.

I especially wanted more wrestling. I had been on the mat only sporadically as I built up my LA client base. Thankfully, Rico had also moved out to LA, and we quickly started collaborating on creating our own training center, which we set up in a beach town warehouse. We focused our club on the emerging sport of Mixed Martial Arts, or MMA. After the 1996 Olympics, Rico and I worked out with Renzo Gracie of Gracie Jiu-Jitsu in his NYC club, back when MMA was in its infancy and wrestlers and Brazilian jiu-jitsu fighters were the dominant forces. We learned pretty fast what wrestlers always knew: lock us in a cage with the toughest guys, and we're going to come out on top. But we also realized that if we could fuse their submission holds and our takedown and pressure skills, our guys could rule the sport. Which we did. With MMA as a focus and Rico's fight management business, called RAW (Real American Wrestling), running on the side, we started making it work. I had designed the fitness elements, installed the equipment, and was setting up to run the personal training…until I came in one Sunday morning with my kids and found out one of the investors had booked our gym out for a girl-on-girl porn shoot to help pay the rent.

That experience made me think about what I was doing. I loved the people I trained, but Hollywood itself started to feel as fake as the breasts on the girls being filmed that day. Then again, who was I to judge? I was just as fake in front of the people I trained, as I gave them the performance they needed from me. And I was one hell of a performer in a town loaded with them. I had impacted a lot of people's lives in a really positive way. The relationships I forged were real and deep and authentic, but they were based on what I wanted them to know. I often thought to myself, *God forbid they should ever know who I really am.* I absolutely didn't want anybody to know. Nobody really wants to be told *I've met God and you haven't,* and

I wasn't willing to open myself up to even my most receptive clients, like Mary McCormack, as much as I found myself wanting to tell her. Sandy had been receptive too, and that uncomfortable morning I'd told Sandy still stuck in my head. Every time I got ready to tell the story of my near-death experience and imagined answering the question *How did you die?* by admitting I injected cocaine, my will to share unraveled.

I get it. There's lots of stuff people don't want other people to know. There's nothing wrong with that, but saying that I was okay with it all? That wasn't okay, and I knew it. I would never be truly reborn and able to live 100 percent authentically until I did. I was living in a truth, but it was a guarded truth in a city filled with people unwilling to hear about anything other than themselves.

I'd had opportunities to reveal myself. A studio executive with a film called *Body Shots* in production called me to begin training Tara Reid, one of the film's stars, and get her in shape. Tara had a reputation as a party girl, yet I got her through her cardio and onto sculpting her body with my daily weight circuit. While we trained, she'd tell me about her nights out at the clubs. I stayed silent. She figured I couldn't relate, and I never let her know any different. She wasn't Sandy Gallin.

But if I didn't own up to the worst parts of me, I could never truly share my story and the message I was sent back to convey: how prayers of love can hold those you love in the light and give them the strength to overcome.

Then, I got the opportunity to try again.

SEEKING WELLNESS

GERRY HARRINGTON WAS A high-powered manager for stars like Nicolas Cage and Sylvester Stallone. He trained with me and also had me install a gym in the Bel-Air mansion he shared with his wife, Angela—whose grandfather, Harry Warner, founded Warner Bros.— and their two daughters. Gerry and Angela argued constantly—okay, they SCREAMED at each other constantly—but it was clear how much they loved each other and doted on their daughters. Besides, Gerry loved to stir the proverbial pot with everyone, especially those he felt close to. At one of his daughter's birthday parties, I ran into my friend and fellow top LA trainer, Greg Isaacs. Greg and I never competed for business. In fact, I think he was the one who pointed *Allure* my way, and we had even toyed with opening a facility together when I came to LA before I rented space of my own. But when Gerry saw us talking, he couldn't resist yelling to the crowd: *Uh-oh, look out, it's the two top LA trainers! It's like a meeting between the Jets and the Sharks. Be careful, everybody, sparks might fly!* James Caan stood in between us and acted like he was going to referee the fight Gerry was hyping.

Angela just rolled her eyes. She knew Gerry only did those things when he cared about someone. Which is why she came to me with tears in her eyes when I showed up for a session and Gerry was not there. She confided in me that she was worried about Gerry. I don't think she sensed anything about my past when she confided in me, or at least she never said so. She just knew Gerry liked me and valued my discretion as a trainer.

And then I told her my story.

This was the first time I'd shared my story, and it was not about me, but about helping someone else—trying to be the selfless messenger of love and light and hope by admitting the worst parts of what I had done. I put my trust in Angela to receive it, and she responded with gratitude. I said I would reach out to Gerry, but before I had the chance, Angela called me in a panic to say that Gerry was not in good shape and was in a hotel room on Sunset Boulevard. *He needs help. Maybe he'll listen to you.*

To my surprise, Gerry took my call, and I did not hesitate. I told him I had been in the hole he was in. I told him everything—everything I had hidden from the world for decades. I never once thought about me as I spoke. I only paused to make sure Gerry was listening and ask him if he wanted to say anything. And when I finished, Gerry said he trusted me. A few days later, he went to get help.

He and I continued to work out together. One day, he decided we should skip our workout and go for a ride in his new silver Ferrari. We drove around the hills, and as we drove, he looked at me. *Hanny, now I know why all these guys like me hire you. You're a professional friend. That's what you are. You're a professional friend, Hanny.*

That's a nice compliment, Gerry, but I'm an exercise scientist.

Don't give me that shit, Hanny. You're a professional friend.

But I knew he was right. Not about my being a professional friend, but about being more than just a friend, just a trainer, just Hanny. I let him have the last word, and when he dropped me off, his words stuck with me. I had a realization. I wasn't a professional friend—and I still didn't know exactly how to remain in the light with my story—but I did have something more than most trainers had. I wanted to do more than just share that gift as the trainer to wealthy stars. I wanted to use all I had learned to connect and reflect the light in people beyond Los Angeles—to help real men and women across the country take their first steps toward better health. The internet offered me the opportunity to do that. I claimed PrivateTraining. com as an online training portal to reach people in need, like the Midwest housewife who was so overweight she was too embarrassed to leave her house and go to a health club, let alone sit with a trainer. I was able to assess her online, figure out what equipment she had access to, give her an exercise prescription, and help her get on track. The site took off, and I began hiring and managing large teams of trainers to help thousands of people reach their goals.

But my experience with Gerry made me realize I was still missing something working in Los Angeles: real connections to real people. The Hollywood life wasn't doing it for me anymore. I thought about opening my own commercial fitness center in Los Angeles; I developed designs and plans, but when I realized I would need investors, I knew I didn't want that. Just like I didn't want my dad putting me through college, I never wanted to be beholden to anyone for money. Kirsten looked at me when I told her we needed to move. But she also knew life in Los Angeles was not for us.

So where? For two people who wanted nothing more than to settle down, we sure sucked at it.

◆◆◆

IF I WERE WRITING the story I wish I'd lived, this would be the point where Kirsten and I found the home of our dreams and lived happily ever after. I would find the right city to parlay my gifts into work that stimulated my heart and mind. I would build on my connection with Gerry Harrington and find others who needed to hear my story to remain in the light. I would find success. But I'm not hiding my story here.

First, we went back to Virginia. My brother-in-law Joe, who led my intervention, called to say he was impressed with the business

I had built in LA and the national media acclaim I had garnered. He was a commercial real estate broker and an entrepreneur developing two prominent golf clubs: a Jack Nicklaus–designed course adjacent to AOL headquarters, and another designed by current pro Johnny Miller. Joe floated the idea to the investors of having me develop and manage high-end fitness facilities out of each property. I was intrigued, especially because I had trained AOL Time Warner president Bob Pittman, whose new headquarters were adjacent to the club's location. When Joe told us the investors were in, I brokered my clients to other trainers for commission, and Kirsten and I bought a house. I even got back into wrestling and coached at American University, as well as a youth club that Connor and Liam participated in.

Seeing them compete rekindled the fire in me to do the same, and in 2002, at the age of forty-two, I entered the MAWA Folkstyle Open Nationals in Salisbury, Maryland. I wanted to feel wrestling flow through my veins like the drugs I no longer craved. I wanted to release all the pent-up animalistic energy that made me feel so good, so connected to my body. I wanted my boys to see what their old dad could do, just as I had shown Kirsten in 1988. They had been too young to understand the 1996 Olympic trials. This was my chance, and I made the most of it.

The open tournament had two qualifying events, and I ended up winning ten matches to get to the national finals at the Wicomico Arena in Delaware, where I made it to the championship match against a bleach-blond kid who was a two-time national champion in NCAA Division II. He called himself Dwayner. His fans screamed *Dwayner* as he wrestled, driving Kirsten nuts. He was less than half my age. He looked cool with his blonde hair and devil-may-care attitude. Dwayner was also incredibly tough, bucking me out of bounds and defending my shots. One escape point was all he got off of me, but I got nothing on him.

The score was 1–0 with seven seconds left on the clock. I had time for one more shot. I finally cleared his arms and slid in on a single leg, swept around, and dropped him to the mat as the buzzer sounded. It was a cool moment, but not the coolest moment. That was when I heard my name announced during the medal ceremony, and Connor and Liam rushed the stage. *That's my dad!* I heard them scream as they stared up at me from the foot of the stage. That was a dream I never imagined in my days of darkness, when I couldn't believe I would survive another year, let alone have a family and compete again.

Life was good. If I were writing the story I wish I'd lived, I would stop it right there.

When construction lagged for two years at the facilities, the gyms were scrapped, and I found myself out of a job. But I still had connections. I had just met an executive from a DC-based group that managed spas and health clubs internationally, and he told me they had a new contract on a property in South Beach, Florida. They wanted me to become their lead man. It was a great opportunity, we sold our Virginia home and moved into our new beach house while I opened the Flamingo South Beach Athletic Club. Once the club opened, I ran it and several other clubs in and around the Miami region. My boys played tennis in a club every day after school, and we'd play at night when I'd get home.

If I were writing the story I wish I'd lived, I would tell you we lived happily ever after in Miami.

After a few years, I looked to advance my position. If I was going to stay in the commercial health club business, I wanted to work with the best in the category, and that was Life Time Fitness. I wrote the CEO a letter outlining my background and expressing my interest in his company. A senior executive called a week later and flew me up to their headquarters in Minnesota, where they offered me my first job with them, turning around a DC-based club. After I exceeded expectations in the first assignment, I was offered the opportunity to open a new club in Atlanta. If I succeeded, there would be more opportunities to keep growing in the region. We fell in love with

Atlanta and bought a house in the exclusive North Atlanta suburbs of Alpharetta.

If I were writing the story I wish I'd lived, I would tell you we lived happily ever after in Atlanta.

Like everywhere we moved, life was good at first. I even got back into wrestling. I ran into a trainer I knew from New York City, and he told me my old rival Lee Kemp was in town. I contacted Lee, and we began training together. He was still in amazing condition, and we battled much like we had twenty years earlier. We joked that Oprah should do a story on how two guys like us could still fight like this at our age and that nobody would believe it. If he only knew how true those words were for me.

Lee then introduced me to his college roommate and teammate at the University of Wisconsin, John Bardis, the founder and CEO of Atlanta-based MedAssets. John was in as good of shape as Lee, and we hit it off instantly. He soon hired me away from Life Time to create a culture of health and fitness for thousands of employees nationwide as his new director of wellness. I loved the job, especially because it gave me the opportunity to impact the health of thousands, it also allowed me more time with Kirsten and the boys.

OUR ANGEL WRESTLES WITH
ADDICTION

FOLLOWING THE INDIAN OCEAN tsunami of 2004, I heard a story about a mother and her two sons, ages two and five. As the waters rose, they kept moving to higher ground, but the rising and rushing waters soon had them trapped. She clung to her boys, but quickly realized she couldn't hold onto both of them or they all would die. Faced with a "Sophie's Choice" and no time to make it, she let her five-year-old go. He had the best chance of surviving, while the two-year-old would surely drown. She and both of her children survived, but she had no way of knowing that would happen in a natural disaster that killed more than 200,000. She just knew in that moment that she had to hold onto the one who needed the most help.

Before Connor fell into his opioid addiction, if you told us we would have to "let go" of one of our children to save the other, it would have been Connor. He was perfect in the classroom, never hung around with bad kids, and did nothing that raised any red flags. Not that Liam was weak. Liam was just…different. Everything was always a little chaotic around Liam. Some of it was extreme impulsiveness, but a lot of it was just Liam being Liam. School never suited him much unless he was getting in trouble, like during lunch hour in third grade, when he stood on top of the cafeteria tables and engaged in a rap-off with a friend.

Liam was as stubborn as he was loving, always wearing his heart on his sleeve. He was also our little entrepreneur. At ten, he set up a pushcart called Ice Cream and More and positioned it near the neighborhood pool, where it soon became the preferred hangout and source for all things frozen for the teenagers. At age twelve, he launched his own online radio station, Q107. He learned the trade by persuading the big Atlanta stations to let him sit with their DJs as they broadcast their Friday night shows. He even got the attention of the number-one morning show, which had him on as a guest. They called him Kidd Liam. He killed it. They had him on again. He killed it again. They ended up offering him his own show.

Before he was even a teenager, Liam was a master at parlaying every opportunity into another one. He used his radio celebrity to pitch an idea to turn a local roller-skating rink into a monthly teen dance event. He promoted it on social media, handled all the logistics, hired staff and bouncers, arranged for a local police officer in uniform, brought in a headliner DJ, set up sound and lights, and positioned go-go dance boxes around the space. He had soft drinks and glow sticks ready for sale, and when the doors opened, the crowd was enormous. He made a mint that night and at similar events he set up at other Atlanta venues. As this and every new plan he concocted succeeded far more than it failed, Kirsten and I would shake our heads—*How did he pull this stuff off?*—and hold on for the ride.

Then Connor decided to try wrestling.

Before Connor hit the mat, I made sure it was what he wanted and that he wasn't just trying to please me. Ever since my teammate Sam at Penn State told me how happy he was to be done with wrestling—because his father had made him do it even though he hated it—I kept my vow never to push anyone into anything, let alone my own children. Too many kids whose fathers had done that hated their dads for it—and the sport too. I loved wrestling. I found joy in competing. I left it because I believed I couldn't compete, and I didn't love it more than the drugs anymore. I came back because it gave me the challenge and fulfillment I needed, and I missed it whenever I stopped. Connor hadn't wrestled since we moved to Virginia, but he assured me his return was for him, not for me. He made the high school team.

The broken leg he suffered that season could have happened to anyone. Nothing unusual. He got wrapped up by his opponent, lifted, and slammed. I had seen that plenty of times. Connor just landed awkwardly. He moved to keep fighting but couldn't stand or walk. The match was called. Twenty-four hours later, he had a big cast and a bottle of Oxycontin,—a prescription to kill the pain that turned into a prescription for addiction.

It was Liam who partially opened our eyes to what was going on with Connor. He told us he smelled Connor smoking pot. We confronted Connor. I was naive and resigned to it just being a problem with weed but Kirsten sensed it was more. She relentlessly searched his room, even searching the ceiling tiles and opening his Time Capsule—a first-grade project that was sealed and not supposed to be opened by him until his twenty-first birthday. There it was hiding in the decorated old Pringles canister, a few pain killer meds and cough syrup. He admitted to a deeper addiction to Oxy, and to getting pain meds from kids at school. He had gone from honor student athlete to full-blown passed-out-in-our-hallway-unable-to-make-it-all-the-way-to-his-bed addict in a matter of months.

I thought back to the night I could not confront the rocker who hit his girlfriend. My inability to act. The helplessness I felt. The disgust. The loneliness. The path that led to my near-death experience. I felt like an idiot for missing and denying the signs, and I resolved not to have those same feelings when facing my son.

Kirsten was adamant about putting him in treatment, he was not yet eighteen and we still had a window of time to force him to go. I committed to doing everything we could to save Connor's life.

It turned out his first stint in rehab was where his roommate taught him how to get and shoot heroin instead of chasing pills. Things escalated, as did our efforts to save him. We hospitalized him, sent him to treatment and rehab centers, and got him into sober living homes and solutions programs—little of it covered by insurance. We wiped out our savings and mortgaged our future to the tune of hundreds of thousands of dollars in medical bills. We filed for Chapter 7 bankruptcy to discharge the debt and keep treating Connor, but he kept relapsing harder and harder, and nothing led to recovery. As graduation banners were being hung around the neighborhoods for kids his age going off to college, we were in a world of hurt, no one we knew could relate to our desperate situation. Then one doctor strongly advised us to get him out of Atlanta and away from his fellow users and drug dealers. Kirsten was exhausted—emotionally and mentally broken down, her faith tested from caring for Connor and making sure nothing happened to Liam while I worked to make ends meet—but she agreed that what we were doing wasn't working. I still had some connections in California and quickly arranged for a job to try and revive the flagging fortunes of a large health club there, only telling them that we had decided to explore new opportunities on the Left Coast.

A few days later, we walked away from our lives in Atlanta — packed an RV, hitched our car to the back, pulled Liam from the first school he was truly thriving in, and headed across the country. We weren't just letting go of Liam. We were letting go of everything we had to hold onto Connor.

CALIFORNIA DREAMING & REALITY

CONNOR SHOOK AND SUFFERED from withdrawal as we drove, drowsy and out of it from the prescription Suboxone Kirsten gave him at prescribed intervals to mitigate the painful withdrawal symptoms. I wanted to believe he wanted to live, to break from the shackles of despair that come with drug dependency. I remembered the same feelings, and the loneliness I felt when I wrote those notes for my family to be found when the cops searched my dead body. At least Connor was not alone, as I had made myself then. But Kirsten and I felt isolated.

Like the whole story of my addiction, death, and rebirth, we did not share our suffering even with the people closest to us. When Bruce Weber's office called two days into our journey to offer me an Abercrombie shoot in the Hamptons (he wanted me to choreograph an athletic wrestling-themed shoot), I said I was not available. They increased the fee, but I couldn't do it at any price. I couldn't leave Connor and abandon Kirsten, and I believed I couldn't explain why. Hiding it from Bruce, who had seen me in the throes of my own struggle, meant there was no one I trusted to share what was going on with except the people who could directly help Connor.

We had tried to be transparent about it with other parents and people in the community we called our friends. They stopped hanging out or communicating with us. We told ourselves we didn't need their judgment and the pain that came with it. I even resisted calling for help when a tire blew out, shredding the RV wheel well and stranding us for hours on the side of a mosquito-infested highway.

This is why so many families like ours feel alone when dealing with addiction, get tested to the limits of their love (as Kirsten and I had been), and sadly fall apart (which we fought not to do). We lose ourselves in the isolation and pain. We feel no one will listen without judgment or some misguided desire to fix our problem. But we don't need fixing. We need people to listen and provide unconditional love. There is nothing harder in life, even when the stakes are much lower. Support groups provide only so much solace unless you find one for families. Most are filled with well-meaning people who want to help, but they are mostly recovering addicts themselves, not families dealing with addicts. You feel disconnected and long to just get back to your child's side.

We arrived in California and parked the RV at a Newport Beach campground near the three-story Ultra Sport Club that had hired me as GM—the largest health club on the West Coast. Kirsten took the lead with Connor and Liam, finding the treatment Connor needed and enrolling Liam at Newport Harbor high school. That first night, Liam pulled a Liam, convincing the manager of a nearby beach hotel to let him become the DJ at its beachside bar. A local bike shop crafted a tow trailer for Liam's bike to transport his gear and his Kidd Liam banner. The same night Liam met with that manager, I drove Connor to an NA meeting at the beach, and we immediately learned why Newport Beach had a reputation as a haven for people in our situation. We found ourselves surrounded by young people like Connor, looking to recover.

We believed California had hit the reset button for us. Hope filled our bodies each day Connor added to his sobriety. He went to meetings every day and passed his urine tests. We found a rental on Newport Beach and sold the RV. I was working seven-day weeks and ten-to-twelve-hour days, the only celebrity client I saw in my club was Kobe Bryant who came to get a workout on our basketball court during the NBA strike. Every night I came home, I felt better and better. Kirsten and I would bike along the beach or just stand outside our beachfront apartment every evening and smile. One night, we biked by the beachfront mansion that had hired DJ Kidd Liam and watched the guests dancing.

But life was not a party. Kidd Liam was doing great, but Liam the kid was struggling academically and mentally. Leaving Georgia had been a big disruption for him. He'd had his best year at a private school in Georgia prior to our California exodus, and he wasn't doing well at his new school. We had let go of him too long while holding onto Connor, who was doing great after six months sober, had a job, and proclaimed himself ready to move into a sober living home on his own. The club I managed was back above water, now exceeding monthly budget goals and sporting solid staff morale.

Another month went by, and things were not any better for Liam. We knew what we had to do: let go of Connor, help him move into a sober living home and make his own way. We needed to leave Connor behind in California for Liam's sake. I contacted Life Time Fitness, and they offered me a relocation package and management position to return to Atlanta. I accepted.

As we prepared to pull up stakes once more, Kirsten began to sense that Connor might be using again. He had passed the urine tests, but she could not shake her motherly gut feeling that something was wrong. Still we continued our preparations. We had subleased the apartment, put the furniture in storage until moving day, and flown Liam back to stay with friends and enroll in his old school. Connor, Kirsten, and I checked into a hotel for a few days to get him settled in his sober living home before we made the drive across the country. Yet Kirsten could not shake the feeling that something was wrong. She cried constantly every time she thought about it. She cried when we checked into the hotel. She would cry as she lay on the bed in her clothes until she fell asleep. She felt helpless, and I couldn't help her because I believed everything was okay. Me, the addict—the one who should have known, should have had the same gut feeling. But I didn't.

The day before Connor was set to check into the sober house, Kirsten decided to take a dip in the pool to relax. That's when Connor came to me and said he needed to go to the hospital. He showed me an infection on his arm that looked like encephalitis or MRSA. He had a fever and looked gaunt. I told Kirsten to come up, and we took him to the nearest ER at UC Irvine. The waiting room was packed with people, including a woman in labor on a stretcher.

We decided to take our chances and drive to a small hospital in Laguna Beach. Connor was put in a room right away. The first thing he asked for were pills for the pain. Following strict HIPPA protocol, the hospital put Connor on IV antibiotics and painkillers and told us nothing except to come back if his fever went up too high. Kirsten called Connor's sponsor and told him she was concerned. I, on the other hand, still believed Connor. Even when Connor's fever spiked late that night, I believed it was just an infection. I had to meet the moving truck at the storage unit at 7:00 a.m., I told Kirsten she had to drive him to the ER herself. She was furious with me but wasted no time arguing. She thought the UC Irvine ER would be less crowded at midnight and, not wanting to drive to Laguna Beach on her own, told me she would take him there.

They admitted Connor immediately. The doctor assigned to him happened to be the head of the addiction unit, and as he examined Connor, he looked at Kirsten. *Tell your mom the truth.* He waited. *Tell your mom that your infection is from a very recent injection site. Tell her that's where you hit yourself up. Tell her now, because you have an abscess in your arm, and if the clot goes to your lungs, heart, or brain, you could die.* Connor looked at Kirsten, and his eyes told her everything.

Kirsten was right. Connor had been using for weeks.

When Kirsten called to deliver the news, she was beyond angry at me for not being there, not trusting her gut, missing the signs again, and leaving her alone to deal with the pain of discovery. The only one more furious at me was me. But we had no time to fight. We had to figure out what to do. Delaying the move was not an option, the moving truck had just departed with our belongings. Delaying my job was not an option. Delaying dealing with Connor, who now lay shivering from fever and withdrawal on the hotel bed, was not an option. *Should we split our family up, and have Kirsten stay with Connor in California? Should we just leave and take Connor with us back to Atlanta?*

When he heard that, Connor sat up, glassy-eyed from the painkillers. He was adamant that he was going to stay in California, bike to his job at the suntan store, and deal with his addiction in the sober living home. We left an urgent message for the director of the home Connor was supposed to arrive at that day to ask for his advice.

As Kirsten and I waited for the call back and continued to argue, nothing made sense to us. She bore the brunt of the suffering, I apologized, we dropped to our knees, embraced each other, and prayed in sorrow as Connor looked on from his bed. As we stood up, the phone rang. It was the manager of the sober home; he was on his way over. He sat with Connor and arranged to go to a meeting with him that night. We extended our stay at the hotel for one more night. We were still up waiting for Connor when he returned from the meeting with a new white Narcotics Anonymous chip and renewed hope to move forward. We looked at the manager and decided to trust him to watch over our son.

The next day, we took Connor to the home and met his new housemates, fellow addicts all. A jaundiced young man welcomed us, and seeing our stares told us he was suffering from the Hepatitis C he caught from sharing infected needles, but he was clean now. There was just no cure for Hep C yet. None of what we saw and heard made us feel better, but we had no choice. I pulled my bicycle out of my pickup truck and left it for Connor as his only means of transportation, and hugged him as tight as I could. We knew it was time to let go and hope Connor could swim on his own.

As Kirsten and I said our tearful goodbyes, Connor smiled and told us how much he loved us. As I looked into his eyes, I thought about the first time I had ever looked into those eyes and how his light filled my world. I wondered if this would be the last time it did.

◆◆◆

THE NEXT DAY, I hitched my pickup truck to a U-Haul trailer that towed our Chevy sedan, picked up Kirsten, and started our trip home as the sun began setting on the Pacific. I wondered if it was a metaphor for our relationship and our son. As we climbed through the beautiful California mountains, we looked out on the beauty of the world, watching it fade into darkness, unable to speak. *How can things be so painful in this beautiful setting?* We wondered what it was like to be normal parents. We couldn't even look at each other because of the pain we both carried, thinking of Connor. Every time we tried, the rawness of our emotions made us recoil. We prayed, but not together, me out loud and her in silence. I looked at Kirsten as we drove, but most of the time she wore headphones and couldn't hear me even if I tried to speak. We couldn't even listen to music together.

Kirsten later told me she pretty much listened to the same song over and over—"Black is the New Yellow" by Super8 & Tab. Connor gave her the song. She loved it even more for its connection to him. She felt drawn to it. It was her way of coping, the way wrestling had been for me. But she also called it the loneliest song you will ever hear. And we were the loneliest couple, not able to even smile or have a laugh. I think our connection on the drive would have been the same if Kirsten sat in the Chevy we towed. We struggle even today to describe the sadness we felt then—the feeling of loss, even though we hadn't lost Connor yet. The silence between us said it all. The one thing we had always had—always forced each other to have—

was hope. Kirsten gave me that. She refused to give it up, no matter how hard things got. I didn't see that hope in her now. Just the same numbness I felt as we sped away from Connor and toward Liam. It was the lowest we got as a couple. We felt helpless.

As we approached Georgia, our mood shifted a little. We finally laughed together as we talked about all those perfect families with their graduation banners, *we should have hung one proclaiming Connor's completion of the Ridgeview Treatment Center*. We remembered how lucky we were to still have each other. The sight of spring filled the car windows and perfumed the air, lifting our spirits. We knew we had to be present for Liam and resolved to believe the best. For the first time in days, we prayed together for Connor. We couldn't get our old house back, so we stayed with the same friends who put up Liam for a couple of days and found a rental house in time for the moving truck's arrival. We spoke to Connor on and off as we settled in. I started work on time and was tasked with getting the club back in shape, driving the team to sell a "daily need" of memberships. But my real daily need was to know my prayers for Connor to recover once and for all would be there for him even if he crossed over into death, as I had twenty-seven years earlier.

It was about two weeks later when Connor called us and said if he didn't come home, he was going to die. Raised Catholic, it was hard for us to miss the connection between what Connor said and the fact that it was Good Friday—and that we would need a miracle for our son's resurrection. It had been a rapid and progressive path to his continuing use in California. Heroin was everywhere—even at the sober house he lived in, where everyone was using. The owner was never there. The manager we'd trusted had no control. Connor told us he had contracted Hepatitis C sharing needles with the jaundiced boy we met the first day.

We picked up the yellow skeleton of our son at the airport on Easter Sunday, a few days before we met with the psychiatrist who told us to plan for Connor's funeral. It turned out Connor had shot up the rest of his heroin in the bathroom at John Wayne Airport in Orange County and disposed of his needles and other paraphernalia before clearing security for his connecting flights through Chicago and Charlotte. I met him alone curbside at the Atlanta airport and hugged him the way I did when he was a child.

My son was alive, but he was far from resurrected. He went to meetings, which was where he hooked up and started using again in Atlanta. Later, a "friend" we had met at the California sober living home called Connor and asked to come to Atlanta. Connor said the friend desperately needed help and had nowhere to go, and we knew what that home was like. I spoke with the friend by phone, and he said all the right things about how committed he was to sobriety. So we flew him in, and we ended up bringing a fellow user into our home. We thought they were going to meetings, but they were using drugs at the Bluff, a notorious Atlanta drug spot. I promptly kicked that kid out and gave him a one-way flight to go find his parents back in Ohio.

After this comes the event that opened this book: the doctor asking if we had planned Connor's funeral, the hospitalization for his Hep C, us thinking we had done everything we could to save him. Realizing he was still using, we registered him with a methadone clinic as a last resort.

The pain and conflict of those days fell hard on Kirsten. But what could I do? I had started managing my new club and spent fourteen-hour days making it run properly. If it went under, we would have no money to help Connor. I had no time to wrestle or work out, but at least I was out of the house. Kirsten was taking every gut punch Connor dished out as he kept using. We had mortgaged our life again. Kirsten was falling apart trying to keep our home together, and I wasn't there for her. We were both suffering in silence. We were living together, but we weren't a typical husband and wife, because there was too much sadness and stress, as she bore the burden of doing the next right thing to help Connor while also keeping hold of Liam. When we did speak, we fought out of mutual frustration.

217

It took seeing my son so close to death to finally make me break down and tell Connor the story of how I lost but regained my life. All of it. I made him listen to the pieces he knew and the depths he didn't. If I thought I knew what it was like to feel vulnerable taping up my injuries as a wrestler, I had no idea.

LIVING IN THE LIGHT

DADS ARE SUPPOSED TO be heroes, and here I was taking myself down in front of my son like no opponent ever did on the mat. Dads are supposed to be strong, but here I was showing how weak I was. Dads can't understand what kids are going through, but here I was telling my son I not only knew what he was going through, but had taken one step further into the beyond. I also told him about my regret that after seeing the light, I didn't take up my dad's offer for rehab and treatment. I knew I was still an addict—just as I know I am today, despite being sober. Instead of seeking healing then, I kept running without fully facing my past. As a result, it took me years with the strength of knowing my Creator to get completely clean. It wasn't until I basked in the glow of Kirsten's love that the worst part of my addiction ended, and when Connor and then Liam's lights entered my world, it was gone for good. He and his brother helped me fight the darkness that can always, *always* return. I did not want him to wait as long as I did to see the light.

Connor told me that while he knew I had shared with him and in group meetings that I too was an addict, that wasn't the same as hearing the story. Knowing how I wrestled with angels as they ripped my soul from my overdosed body made it easier for us to relate to each other. Did knowing this make Connor better right away? Of course not. But, as Connor said, even as far gone as he was, what kept him alive sometimes was knowing he could come back to me—the very thing that kept me alive, the love that anchored me to this world the day I met my maker. When he hit the lowest of the lows, I was still there to talk about what was going on in truth, transparency, and light. Connor had to find his own path, but he could find it now knowing I was on the path with him, holding him in the light.

Kirsten stuck with him for everything else and hired a highly respected interventionist to help convince Connor to truly surrender and check-in to a residential treatment center in Florida. During the intervention, Kirsten went to a church and prayed, she told me she lit a candle in the chapel and then sat on a beautiful ornate bench outside the church. A priest who spoke no English approached as she sat there in tears. He put his hand on her head and kept it there for a long time as he prayed. *I don't know what he did,* she told me, *I was just crying, and he stood there praying silently, it was as if he knew and suddenly a sense of calm came over me like it was going to be all right.*

I called Kirsten as the priest left her, and I told her Connor was on his way to the airport.

The renowned interventionist helped save Connor but sadly it turned out she was also a suffering addict and killed herself soon after. Her effort connected us with a treatment center in Florida that somehow clicked for Connor. Kirsten's gut also told her something was different. The place was awful, his therapist seemed disconnected, but Connor was so happy. He was content to be off of drugs. Kirsten arranged to borrow money from her mother to make it happen, and then lined Connor up to do a new treatment at Atlanta's Emory Hospital for his Hep C, if he made it through the rehab.

He did. Something changed within Connor while he was in Florida, and with Kirsten and me too. By the grace of God we had survived to this point. I now fully understood the power of the light I had been given. I saw that the power of my story—like *all* our stories—could help strengthen and heal when offered from a place of selflessness, courage, truth, and love. It pains me to think that if I understood this earlier—before Connor broke his leg, before the addiction, before he OD'd for the first time, before Kirsten and I tested every ounce of faith we had in ourselves and each other— that I might have saved us some of the pain we are still recovering from. That we will always be recovering from, as we rebuild our love into something different but eventually stronger. Every day I wonder, *What if I had shared my story before any of this happened, to give Connor a tool to live and change his story—to give him a different way of looking at life?*

When we look back, Kirsten, Connor, and I see so much hurt and struggle—within ourselves, with each other, and with others. Could we have avoided that? None of us think it would have prevented Connor's addiction. But Connor says that while hearing my story earlier would not have stopped or cured him, he knows he wouldn't have survived without hearing it. It made him a stronger person even when he was just about as low as he could possibly be. A person who wanted to have a longer story to tell. A son who wanted to come home.

Connor has been clean since April 2012. He gave me permission and encouraged me to share his story, as I finally gave myself permission to share mine. I have been completely free from the shackles of drugs for over twenty-six years. Not that the years since have made all this any easier to look back on; uncomfortable truths are never easy to confront. Connor and I know we still face tremendous challenges to remain on the well-lit path, but now we have each other to stay the course.

We also know no one gets through life unscathed, and while everyone has their own unique story, we don't wish what we went through on anyone. Especially a parent. Watching a child go through what Connor did changes you forever. We are healing, but we don't feel we will ever be the same. We know addiction affects more families and people than we—and you—can imagine. So if my story (and Connor's) can help save one life or help one family open up to the love and light inside and around them and live their stories in that light, in hope and prayer and energy, it's worth the pain I felt putting this on paper.

The scourge of opioid addiction, in all its forms, is real. We need to talk about it. It's a powerful disease that does not discriminate by class or race or ethnicity or gender or where you live. A hit of heroin still costs less than the price of a six-pack, and it's about as easy to find. We've seen it in the city and the suburbs. An old wrestling buddy of mine lives in upstate New York, and he's seen customers at the working-class stiff bar he goes to shooting up in the back. It has taken our children. Connor knows more people than he can count on his hands who have died from heroin or another opioid derivative. From 1999 to 2018, a total of 770,000 Americans died from drug ODs. That's more precious souls than were lost in the entire Civil War. More deaths in that period than all of America's other wars combined: WWI, WWII, Korea, Vietnam etc. These *deaths of despair* as they are categorized by the NCHS, have caused a drop in our nation's life expectancy.

There are many ways to deal with addiction, but *deal* with it you must. My greatest hope is that my story helps you share yours, so you can help another who might be struggling or help someone understand your struggle in full truth and honesty, so you can reflect the light we all have inside and around us. In the end, my story offers only one lesson: you cannot do it alone.

I became the complete messenger I was meant to be when I met Connor in the light of truth and love. I remembered how the loneliness overwhelmed me, drowned out my prayers, made me feel helpless—made me feel *hopeless*—and pushed me deeper into darkness, until I came as close as humanly possible to the point of no return. I shared my story with Connor because I knew his loneliness had done what it did for me: left him with nothing but despair.

I knew it would take more than my story to save Connor, just as it took more than one prayer to hold him in the light. I knew we would have to keep sharing and praying and loving for him to hear me, but finally he did.

If you are going through this, know we hear you. Remember the message I was sent back to convey: how prayers of love can hold those you love in the light and give them strength. Know that even if your loved one has tragically passed, your prayers have not gone unseen, as my parents' prayers were seen by me when I passed over and went to a better place.

CODA
THE DREAM & THE REALITY

YEARS BEFORE, WHEN I hadn't fit wrestling in because I was working long days to satisfy the corporate pressure to produce—days when I didn't even leave time for a workout—I felt stressed and empty. Those days, I prayed for the strength to get through it all, and although we felt weak, God somehow gave us enough strength to make it through.

Connor has since never relapsed, and has not only worked his way back to health, but is also now in London, where he finished his degree in film and is pursuing a career making movies. His constant willingness to let the light in him shine inspired me to let mine burn bright too, on the mat. So in the years following Connor's recovery, I never completely left wrestling again.

I launched my own health and wellness company and also returned to training athletes in Atlanta. I worked out MMA and UFC fighters. I won the southeast region USA Grappling World Team Trials tournament in submission wrestling. I love training others toward their goals, but I also began competing and training hard for myself. It was about control for sure, but it wasn't about adulation or addiction anymore. It was a place where I went to de-stress, share fellowship, feel good, and keep moving—to keep fighting any temptation to violate my sobriety in good, boring, and bad times. I wasn't using wrestling to run away, though at times it might have looked like that to Kirsten. I would always wrestle when things got tough and life tested my resiliency. But I always ran back home. It was my spiritual connection to conquering life's struggles. My family was my temple.

Then the governing body of Olympic wrestling began holding the annual United World Wrestling Championship for veteran wrestlers in various host cities around the world, and I realized I still had a chance to live one of my dreams. My NCAA national championship dream died my senior year. My dream to represent my country in the Olympics fell short for good in 1996. But here was a chance to be a world champion and a winner while living in my light, my truth, for my family. For me.

To honor the fact that Connor and I had both been completely sober for a number of years, I went for it. I flew to Athens to compete, and came up short again, winning three bouts but then losing to a four-time Olympian, José Betancourt from Puerto Rico. Leave it to wrestling to always keep you humble. But I wasn't humiliated, as I had been in the past. I was determined. I knew it was going to take more work from my fifty-six-year-old ass to do this. More cardio. More strength training. More wrestling. I trained the next year straight for the 2016 championships, which were scheduled in Poland. I liked the idea of winning there, coming full circle in the place my international career began as a junior champion forty years before.

I tested my progress at the US nationals in Las Vegas for veterans six months after Athens, pinning a world medalist in the finals in just thirty-nine seconds. No one scored a point on me. Still, after the tournament, people were telling me that I didn't have a chance to beat Willem Putter in Poland. *Johnny, you'll never beat Putter. Johnny, he's a ten-time world champion. Johnny, he's a legend, he's a monster.*

I didn't care. I was doing everything I knew how to do this time to prepare. I researched him and looked for weaknesses others had missed. I noticed he was very strong, with solid head and hands defense, and just swept people to the side. That's when I developed my game plan. I would start out by just jolting him—take him out of his comfort zone. I would resist over-attacking, because he could counter score with his defense, which was how he won most of his matches. I just needed one good takedown. If I got that out of the gate, I would make it stand. It would make for a boring match, but I remembered what Lee Kemp had taught me: a great champion can have many weapons, but should never put himself at risk of losing when the stakes are high.

I wasn't going to let pride and any lingering need for putting on a good show keep me from listening to Kemp's advice and realizing my dream. The fact that I would have my friend, employer, wrestling's generous benefactor, and Olympic team leader John Bardis in my corner made it easier to stay determined. Bardis was Kemp's roommate at the University of Wisconsin. After I told him about my loss to Betancourt, he said, *You are going to win it next year, and I'm going to be in your corner.* I didn't think he meant it. But he did, and it felt amazingly cool that he would put everything aside and be my corner coach in Poland.

I put on a good show in my first matches, beating a German 6–0, a Hungarian 6–0, and another German 10–0. But when it was time for Putter, who had equally laid waste to his opponents to get to the championship, I followed my plan. *Whistle. Jolt. Hammer down, attack, attack, snap and score. Takedown for Johnny! Protect. Protect. Protect. Move. Move. Stay on the attack. Whistle! 2–0 Win. World Champ!*

Dream fulfilled. Light fully reflected.

If you look at the picture of my arm being raised in victory on the mat, I am not smiling. Sure, I'm exhausted, but I also think the full realization of what I had finally accomplished hadn't hit me. And then it did. And I smiled and let all the light out. I smiled thinking of my team, my family, my kids, and Kirsten. I smiled thinking about myself. I'd never felt a smile like this. Bardis saw it too and snapped a picture that I cherish. You don't need to see the energy around me to know that it's there. You feel it in that photo.

That energy continued to run through me as I pulled on my running shoes and my USA warm-up and headed over to the staging area for the medal ceremony. I was feeling pretty good. Actually, I felt nothing but the buzz running through my body, which vibrated at the same frequency as the bright red arena. I'd seen these ceremonies on TV and from the stands at the Olympics, but I could never imagine the buzz—this rush of feeling as I waited to be called to the podium. I took my place next to Putter. I nodded respectfully. I was trying to act like I'd been here before, and I had—over and over in my dreams. I'd played it all out in my mind. Used the dream to maintain my winning mindset after I failed in 1984 and walked away from wrestling for the first time. Used it to motivate myself for the last year—to endure the pain and push through the mundane days, to put in the work I wasn't willing to do when cocaine polluted my body.

Looking for something to divert my attention, I watched three young women walking up beside me, dressed in flowing white blouses with blue trim, long red skirts, and what looked like white aprons that must reflect a Polish tradition. The strange juxtaposition of our warm-ups and sweating bodies and their decorative dresses and pretty makeup allowed me a momentary distraction…until my eyes locked on the decorative pillows in their arms. Three of them: one holding the bronze medal, one the silver, and one holding *my* world gold medal.

This was not a dream.

An usher gestured for us to line up behind the medal maids, and the arena echoed with the announcer's voice. In English with a thick Polish accent, it directed the crowd's attention to the podium. Music swelled as we marched forward against the brilliant blue World Championship backdrop. A teammate handed me the folded American flag I brought in honor of my father, who had died earlier in the year.

That teammate reminded me of the Marine who'd handed me the flag that draped my father's casket as they sent him off with a solemn twenty-one-gun salute at Quantico. The respect they gave my dad at that ceremony made me cry as much as the fact that my father, and now both of my parents, were gone from this earth. He had been strong enough to survive Iwo Jima and hold our family together. He was humble and loyal and had turned down the honor of being buried at Arlington, saying it was too crowded there and he wanted to fully honor the Marine Corp where his career began at Quantico. That was the strength being sent to Heaven now. The Marines solemnly folded the American flag and handed it to me.

It was an honor to have been his son—an honor I wanted with me in Poland. I knew if I won, I wanted to hold my father with me on top of the podium, so I brought him with me in that flag. As I waited for the ceremony to begin, I remembered that my greatest fear as a kid had been losing my father at an early age. I thought about him telling me the parable of the Prodigal Son when I came home to Virginia, broke, alone, directionless, and fighting to stay clean. I wondered now if he had told me that parable and opened his door to me that day because his greatest fear was losing me at a young age. I know that had been my greatest fear when Connor fell into the throes of his addiction.

The last thing I did with my dad, on my last visit to our house before he died, was what he wanted: we prayed. It was the rosary— the same meditative prayer Mom wanted me to do in Boston, when I faced the first crossroads in my relationship with Kirsten. Dad didn't have much time, so I recorded it as a gift to my brother and sisters, so we could share the prayer and Dad's calming affect whenever we needed it. The last words I said to him were *I love you*—something I had found hard to say over the years.

The memories calmed me as a distinguished-looking man in a suit took over from the usher and led us toward the spotlight and the three boxes, the one for gold elevated and flanked by the ones for silver and bronze. We each stood behind the box corresponding to our achievement. The announcer boomed the name of the German bronze medalist, and he jumped easily up onto his podium box. As Putter was announced, my eyes followed him as he made the slightly more difficult climb to his perch. I looked at the gold box again, and it dawned on me that I had one more challenge: to climb to the top of the box when my name was announced.

And now, from the United States, the gold medal goes to John Hanrahan.

I didn't hesitate. I moved with the quickness of the first match of the day and pushed off the floor. I hit the silver medalist's box with one foot and transitioned the rest of my body to the top of the gold medal stand. I heard the roar of the American contingent fill the air above the rest of the applause, and Bardis's booming voice yelled, *Way to go, Johnny!* I raised my arms to acknowledge their cheers, and then bowed as far forward as I could as the dignitary took the gold medal from the woman's pillow and draped its colorful ribbon around my neck. I stood upright. The medal felt impossibly heavy, as if it had taken all the weight from my shoulders. I saw the flags on the other end of the arena, with the American flag fixed in the middle above the other two. The thick accent of the announcer boomed again.

And now, the national anthem of the USA. I placed my right hand over my heart and smiled. I remembered the first time I saw this scene. Black-and-white TV, age twelve, the 1972 Munich Olympics.

I'm a long way from being that kid now.

I'm in a place where I don't have the fear of being scrutinized for the addict I was. The son who refused his parents' help, prayers, and love. The callous one-night-stand lover who was afraid of commitment. The wrestler who walked away more than once as a loser who betrayed himself and his teammates. The star model who lived for his addiction. The man who became the pinnacle of health and trained some of the biggest stars and moguls in the world, but never shared the story of how he polluted himself and caused his own death. The man who almost threw away the love of his life because he had to learn to share control. The man who, despite his own experience, failed to recognize the addiction destroying his firstborn son and to share the light that freed him from addiction.

No more. I feel free to share my story now. Whatever consequences or judgment that may bring, I'm comfortable with it, just as I'm comfortable continuing to wrestle after living my dream. I tell people I'm done competing. I'll wrestle in the room for a workout and help coach the young guys. Kirsten just laughs. She envisions me parking my walker by the side of the mat.

It scares her sometimes. I might get hurt. She knows it might never end and will admit grudgingly that it probably shouldn't. It's the way I deal with life. Our wrestling club has become a fellowship of good-hearted wrestlers of all ages. That fellowship is part of my sobriety, a positive addiction. I wish she had something similar during our fight to save Connor—and now Liam.

Just as Connor is taking his recovery to the next level, living in London to find what he is meant to be, the other light of my life, Liam, has started dealing with his own challenge. He fell into drugs as a young DJ contracted to do a national show tour. I needed him to know I understood what he was going through—how scary the future can seem to a young man, how you can never see where you are going to be years from now, and how you will make it in this world. But you are going to make it if you surrender and seek help. He left the tour and entered treatment.

I understood. *I knew.* And I didn't make the same mistake twice. As Liam was in treatment, I sent him an early draft of this book. Before I showed it to anyone else besides Kirsten and Connor, I needed to tell Liam. I could tell him how much I loved him and was proud of him, but sharing my story would show him.

Show him how unique and full of life he is, and that his mother and I know he has a special purpose to share with the world.

Liam has completed a long stint of residential treatment and is now embracing his sobriety. We pray and we have faith—faith in each other, and that our prayers will hold us all in the loving light, as my parents' prayers held me.

Prayers that the countless others dealing with addiction don't extinguish their hope and faith.

Let your stories and prayers shine and hold us in the light.

I know now that it wasn't Connor who was my ultimate redemption, and Liam won't be, either. I know it will not be Kirsten, even when we finally reclaim, rebuild, and renew our hope in, faith in, and love for each other—everything we have lost in ourselves and with each other in trying to heal our boys. This book is my redemption. I own my message of light through the darkness. Of hope and faith. Of prayer.

So please know, if you are suffering, someone is listening. Someone is praying for you, holding you in that light.

ACKNOWLEDGMENTS

Thank you to Robert Moore, who has had a positive effect on so many lives, and who encouraged me to teach and coach and to share our story of overcoming the challenges of addiction. I am forever grateful to coaches Steve Wilcox (HS), Rich Lorenzo (PSU), and Hamid Kermanshah (NYAC), who have had an immense positive impact on my life and the lives of so many others. To former Olympic Team Leader John Bardis, who led me to achieve my UWW World Veteran Championship. To the photographers—Bruce Weber, Stan Malinowski, Knut Bry, Christopher Makos, Yasushi Handa, and others—I have been privileged to work with you. To so many inspiring individuals who allowed me into their lives to devise and direct their personalized fitness program. To my beautiful wife Kirsten and our two sons Connor and Liam—my love and gratitude for having you to share my life is overwhelming. To my mother Louise and father Donald and my five siblings: Patrick, Donna, Kitty, Teri, and Nancy: thank you for your prayers and for always being there for one another. Your prayers helped save my life.

ABOUT THE AUTHOR

BORN IN WASHINGTON, DC, John Hanrahan is a nationally acclaimed trainer and an NSCA certified strength and conditioning specialist. He is a UWW World Champion in freestyle wrestling and was a two-time NCAA All-American wrestler at Penn State University. He provides health and wellness solutions and education to corporations, athletes, students, and the general public. He and his wife Kirsten have founded RecoveryAngel.org a 501c3 non-profit formed to assist addicts and their families with support and guidance toward recovery. Hanrahan's author website is JohnHanrahan.com, and his wellness site is PrivateTraining.com.